Memories of our Happy days t

Love from Florrie & Jack.
28/3/70.

D1162860

RECORDING SCOTLAND

RECORDING
SCOTLAND

EDITED WITH NOTES BY

JAMES B. SALMOND, M.A., LL.D.

PUBLISHED FOR THE PILGRIM TRUST

BY

OLIVER AND BOYD

EDINBURGH: TWEEDDALE COURT

LONDON: 98 GREAT RUSSELL STREET, W.C.1

FIRST PUBLISHED 1952

Printed in Great Britain by
McLAGAN & CUMMING LTD., EDINBURGH

INTRODUCTION

S HORTLY after the outbreak of the second world war a project was initiated under the auspices of the Ministry of Labour and National Service and the leadership of Sir Hubert Llewellyn Smith with the double object of providing employment for artists in wartime and of forming a permanent pictorial record of places and buildings of beauty and historical interest in Great Britain which were exposed to the hazards of warfare and utilitarian encroachment. The Pilgrim Trustees were invited to lend their financial assistance and gladly did so.

A Committee was first appointed to deal with England and Wales, and the history of the work of that Committee is told in the Introduction to the four volumes of *Recording Britain*, published between 1946 and 1948 by the Oxford University Press. The enterprise is now completed by the publication of this fifth volume which is devoted to the recording of Scotland, a task which was entrusted to a separate Committee specially financed by the Pilgrim Trust and composed of Sir James Colquhoun Irvine, K.B.E., F.R.S., Principal of St. Andrews University (Chairman), Captain Alfred E. Borthwick, R.S.A., President of the Royal Scottish Society of Painters in Water Colours, Mr. Reginald Fairlie, R.S.A., LL.D., Sir David Russell, LL.D. and the late Mr. Kenneth Sanderson, W.S., with Miss I. M. E. Bell as Secretary.

The Scottish Committee had special difficulties to contend with. Wartime restrictions prevented access to some areas, and it was not always easy to provide travelling facilities and accommodation for the distinguished and enthusiastic team of artists enlisted. While the comprehensiveness of the survey of Scotland was thus somewhat impaired by the obstacles interposed by the prevailing conditions, 145 pictures in all were bought or presented. They were exhibited in galleries and schools in many parts of the country, and now form a permanent collection of national importance.

Of these pictures 80, representing the work of 47 artists and covering 24 counties, have been selected for reproduction in this volume, which has been edited by Mr. J. B. Salmond, LL.D. In the letterpress he has admirably provided the social and historical background of the places portrayed.

The Pilgrim Trustees welcome the completion of an enterprise in which they have taken a keen interest. They avail themselves of this opportunity to express their thanks and their congratulations to the members of the Scottish Committee and notably to Captain Borthwick, to whom a special debt is due for the time and trouble which he devoted to the Committee's task. They are grateful also to Dr. Salmond for his editorial work and his own contribution to the volume and to Messrs Oliver & Boyd of Edinburgh who have so successfully surmounted the difficulties which attend all publications in these days.

MACMILLAN
Chairman of the Pilgrim Trust

March 1952

CONTENTS

EDINBURGH

FIFE

GLASGOW AND THE WEST

NORTH AND CENTRAL SCOTLAND

SOUTH OF EDINBURGH

ACKNOWLEDGMENTS

THE Editor wishes to acknowledge the courteous permission, given by Publishers, Authors, and Authors' Executors, to quote from the following books:—

Oliver & Boyd: *Old Edinburgh*, by Ian G. Lindsay.

Faber & Faber: *Off in a Boat*, by Neil M. Gunn, and *I Remember*, by J. J. Bell.

A. & C. Black: *Edinburgh*, by Rosaline Masson, and *Scotland Under Trust*, by Robert Hurd.

George G. Harrap: *Fishermen and Fishing Ways*, by Peter F. Anson.

Herbert Jenkins: *The Life of Rear-Admiral John Paul Jones*, by George Preedy.

EDINBURGH

Artists

ROBERT EADIE

ANDREW GAMLEY

MRS CAMERON KAY

SIR JOHN STIRLING MAXWELL, BART.

JAMES MILLER

ROBERT C. ROBERTSON

ALAN IAN RONALD

A. BRUCE THOMSON

G. P. H. WATSON

ALEXANDER ZYW

BAKEHOUSE CLOSE

Robert C. Robertson

The building above the covered entrance to this Canongate Close is known as Huntly House. It was built in 1570 by George, First Marquis of Huntly. This house has an unhappy kind of history. That first Marquis was responsible for the death of the Bonnie Earl o' Moray.

> Foul fa' you Huntly!
> And why did ye so?
> You might hae ta'en the Earl o' Moray,
> And saved his life too.

Huntly's son, who also inhabited this house, was executed at the Cross of Edinburgh in 1649. A happier home in this Close is Acheson House, the one-time residence of Sir Archibald Acheson of Glencairney, a Lord of Session in the days of Charles I. The date of the building is 1633, and the initials of the builder and his wife are to be found above the dormer windows. Also on the house are engraven the crest of 'cock and trumpet', but no harm was done in this case by the owner 'blowing his own trumpet', and it was a peaceful midden-heid on which this cock crew. There is a letter, quoted by Chambers in his *Traditions of Edinburgh*, from Sir James Balfour to Acheson, which is dated from London '9 Apryll 1631', and for the tang of its words is worth reproducing.

'To Sir Archibald Achesone,
    one of the Secretaries of Staite.

Worthy Sir,—Your letters, full of Spartanical brevity to the first view, bot, againe overlooked, Demosthenicall longe; stuffed full of exaggerations and complaints; the yeast of your enteirest affections, sent to quicken a slumbring friend as you imagine, quho nevertheless remains vigilant of you and of the smallest matters, which may aney wayes adde the least rill of content to the ocean of your happiness; quherfor you may show your comerad, and intreat him from me, as from one that trewly loves and honors his best pairts, that now he vold refraine, both his tonge and pen, from these quhirkis and obloquies, quherwith he so often uses to stain the name of grate personages, for hardly can he live so retiredly, in so voluble ane age, without becoming at one tyme or uther obnoxious to the blow of some courtier. So begging God to bless you, 'I am your—   JA. BALFOUR.'

As I write, Acheson House is being used as a Scottish Craft Centre, where are being collected samples of the finest pieces of handicraft still made in Scotland, for the 1951 Festival Exhibition.

Robert C. Robertson

CAMPBELL'S CLOSE, COWGATE

Robert Eadie

This Close was originally named after a certain Rae, but who he was or what he did history does not relate. George Campbell, however, was a decent meal merchant and a Canongate Bailie. When the Bailie was done with this world, his close, and his tenement, the last-mentioned was occupied by several people not undistinguished in Scottish history. Here dwelt the last Archbishop of St. Andrews, Arthur Ross, whom Burnet described as 'a poor ignorant worthless man; but in whom obedience and fury were so eminent, that they supplied all other defects'. Ross was all for James, and not at all for William, and was one of the signatories to that Loyal Address to James, dated 3rd November 1688, which concludes with the pious wish that 'God, in His great mercy, who has so often preserved and delivered your Majesty, will still preserve and deliver you, by giving you the hearts of your subjects and the necks of your enemies'. The Archbishop died in 1704. His daughter, Anne, was the mother of that Lord Balmerino, who was executed for the part he played in the '45.

After Ross had finished with it, the building became the town house of the (13th and later the 14th) Earls of Morton. The 13th Earl, who was Vice-Admiral of Scotland, died in Edinburgh in 1738. The 14th Earl was a very remarkable man, who sat for thirty years as a member of the House of Lords. On many occasions he must have entertained in this house his great friend, Colin MacLaurin, Professor of Mathematics in the University of Edinburgh. But like MacLaurin he had left that city before the entry of the Jacobite Army. In fact he and his wife were in Paris in 1746, where they were both imprisoned in the Bastille, for reasons of which we have no record.

The Earl in time became President of the Royal Society of London, a trustee of the British Museum, and a commissioner on the Annexed Estates. He died in 1768.

Cloth Hall. Cowgate Edinburgh.   Robert Eadie

THE CANONGATE

James Miller

It is to the Augustine canons of Holyrood that we are indebted for the name of this Edinburgh highway. David I gave them a charter to build here, and the Canongate became a Burgh of Regality quite apart from Edinburgh proper. Forming, as it did later, the site for the homes of the gentry of Scotland, the eyes of a great part of Scottish history have gazed from its windows, the feet have sounded on its pavements, the hoofs of horses bearing its famous and infamous characters have rattled over its cobble-stones. But in the year 1817 a new entrance to the city was made by the side of the Calton Hill, the Canongate lost much of its importance, and was allowed to degenerate into something in the nature of a slum. But in our day much has been done to restore many of the old buildings. The central feature shown in the accompanying picture is the Tolbooth, which was built in 1591 as the courthouse and prison of the Burgh of the Canongate. Another house of distinction in the Canongate was Morocco Land, graced by the figure of a Moor, which holds the legend of a one-time citizen, one of whose female relatives became the wife of a Sultan of Morocco. Then there is Moray House, built in Charles I's day, and occupied by Cromwell. It was from a window of this building that Argyll watched Montrose dragged along the highway to prison and death.

> And a Saxon soldier cried aloud:
> Back, coward, from thy place,
> For seven long years thou hast not dared
> To look him in the face.

Queensberry House holds the memory of a Duchess who showed kindness to the poet Gay, who acted as her secretary. Alongside the Tolbooth is the old Church and behind it the Churchyard where rest Adam Smith, Duguld Stewart and Robert Fergusson. Burns sought out Fergusson's grave in 1786, and from the proceeds of the 'Edinburgh' edition of his poems, he erected a headstone, on which with others are carved the words:

> No sculptured marble, here, nor pompous lay,
> No storied urn, or animated bust—
> This simple stone directs pale Scotia's way
> To pour her sorrows o'er her Poet's dust.

CRAIGMILLAR CASTLE

G. P. H. *Watson*

In the high summer of 1929 came King George V and Queen Mary to an Edinburgh, struggling out of the dust of war's aftermath, and, amid the flaunting of many flags, Scotland's Shrine was dedicated, and Scotland's story told in a pageant at Craigmillar Castle in which several of the parts were played by the descendants of the folk they represented. And a wonderful back-cloth and stage did the old castle and its grounds provide. The original building was of the thirteenth century, but it has suffered much devastation and much reconstruction. In its dungeons was held that much-escaping Prince, the Duke of Albany, James III's brother; but his other brother, the Earl of Mar, died here in as unpleasant a manner as his goalers could devise. In the great hall, with its eleven-foot-wide fireplace, Mary, Queen of Scots, danced in her happy days, and was imprisoned at the beginning of her weary ones. In those happy days the castle could not hold all her folk, so she lodged her servants in a hamlet nearby, which is known to this day as 'Little France', and is in the neighbourhood of the Old Dalkeith Road, where the Queen is said to have planted a sycamore. So much for the stories we know, and so to one of which there is no record. In 1813 during some excavations of the dungeons of Craigmillar, a human skeleton was found built upright into one of the walls.

This morning in making my way to this room in which I am writing, I passed by the walls of the hall of our old college. A well-known Scottish Sheriff was once in a company moving through the quadrangle, when one of that company remarked on the excellent condition of the stone-work. 'I should know how good it is,' said the Sheriff. 'You see, I was the mason.' He had worked there earning money which was one day to 'put him through' that same college. When I gaze from the distance of Edinburgh's outlying streets at the graciousness of Craigmillar on its green hill, and amongst its leafy trees, I am reminded of that other Scottish stone-mason, finished with his day's work on Niddrie Mansion House, walking in the pleasant evening and noting down how he 'often saw the sun sink over the picturesque ruins of Craigmillar Castle'. That mason was Hugh Millar.

EDINBURGH

Sir John Stirling Maxwell, Bart.

This picture has that suggestion of mist and mystery which shrouds so much of Edinburgh's story, a story founded on that great rude Rock, where some kind of defensive building seems to have stood as far back as any history can go. You will find a building on that Rock in Ptolemy's *Geography*; you will even find claims made that some kind of castle was there in 989 B.C. But the oldest building now in existence on the Rock is Queen Margaret's Chapel, for centuries lost sight of, but now with windows filled with beautiful glass by Strachan, and in use again as a chapel. The first definition in the mist of the years is in the figures of Malcolm Canmore and his Queen dwelling in happiness on the Rock. The Queen's last unhappiness is also there, for to that Castle on the Rock came Edmund, her second son, to tell her that her husband and their eldest boy lay slain at Alnwick. So the Queen's heart broke and she died, while Donald Bane's Highland adherents raged below the Rock. But the kindly mist came down, and her children bore the mortal remains of Margaret underneath its cloak from the Castle, and so across the Ferry, named after the lady, to Dunfermline where they buried her in the abbey which she herself had had founded.

That same mist was to give a dreich welcome to another Queen of Scotland, for it lay thick over the city when Mary of Scots landed at Leith. That same mist hung like a blanket when Alexander III left the Castle to ride to his death at Kinghorn. In mist and darkness Randolph and his men scaled the Rock, and took the Castle from the English. On that Rock they dined at 'The Black Dinner'; the Blue Blanket was embroidered by another Queen Margaret and her ladies; Lady Glamis was burned to death; James VI was born; the Crown Jewels rest; the National War Memorial arises.

THE LOW CALTON AND THE REGENT BRIDGE

Robert Eadie

'The broad and comely approach to Princes Street, from the east, lined with hotels and public offices, makes a leap over the gorge at Low Calton; if you cast a glance over the parapet, you look direct into that sunless and disreputable confluent of Leith Street, and the same tall houses open upon both thoroughfares. This is only the New Town passing overhead above its own cellars; walking so to speak over its own children, as is the way of cities and the human race.' So wrote Robert Louis Stevenson of Waterloo Place and Regent's Bridge. Two communities were passed over by the New Town—one, the village of Dean, which was left with some of its pleasantness; the other this extra-mural burgh of Calton which was reft of all its pleasantness—the little Hermitage of St. Ninian, the Collegiate Church of the Holy Trinity founded in 1462 by Mary of Gueldres, Trinity Hospital, and nearby the Physic Garden, 'the favourite open-day haunt of the literature and the polite flirtation of Edinburgh'. Lord Cockburn has left an excellent description of that Trinity Hospital (*circa* 1830), in his *Memorials of His Time*.

'This', he writes, 'is Trinity Hospital. Time, in its course over Edinburgh, has left no other such picturesque deposit.' And, then, in a footnote: 'In a short time, the place shall know it no more! But the public will be gratified by a railway station. Trinity College Church, too—the last and finest Gothic fragment in Edinburgh, though implored for by about four centuries, will disappear for the accommodation of a railway! An outrage by sordid traders, virtually consented to by a tasteless city, and sanctioned by an insensible Parliament. I scarcely know a more curious instance of ignorant insensibility than the apology that is made for this piece of desecration. It is said that the edifice is to be replaced, exactly as it is, in some better situation. And it is really thought that the Pyramids would remain the Pyramids, or Jerusalem, Jerusalem, provided only their materials were replaced in London. Oxford would be Oxford, though in Manchester, if its stones were preserved. These people would remove Pompeii for a railway, and tell us they had applied it to a better purpose in Dundee.'

Desecration is of all time!

EDINBURGH FROM THE WEST

Andrew Gamley

Still on the spot Lord Marmion stay'd,
For fairer scene he ne'er survey'd.
  When sated with the martial show
  That peopled all the plain below,
  The wandering eye could o'er it go,
  And mark the distant city glow
  With gloomy splendour red;
For on the smoke-wreaths, huge and slow,
That round her sable turrets flow,
  The morning beams were shed,
And tinged them with a lustre proud,
Like that which streaks a thundercloud.
Such dusky grandeur clothed the height,
Where the huge Castle holds its state,
  And all the steep slope down,
Whose ridgy back heaves to the sky,
Piled deep and massy, close and high,
  Mine own romantic town!

So Walter Scott has for ever established that southern point of view from which to appreciate Edinburgh. But equally interesting and inspiring are the views from every other airt—that view from the Fife shore which must have been the one imprinted on the minds of Canmore's Queen; that view from down the Firth which must have been the first impression on the minds of all those French folk who came our historic way; and the view from the west, pictured here, which in its general outline must have met the eyes of Prince Charles Edward Stuart, when he marched on the capital of his fathers from Linlithgow, and before he turned southwards to Slateford.

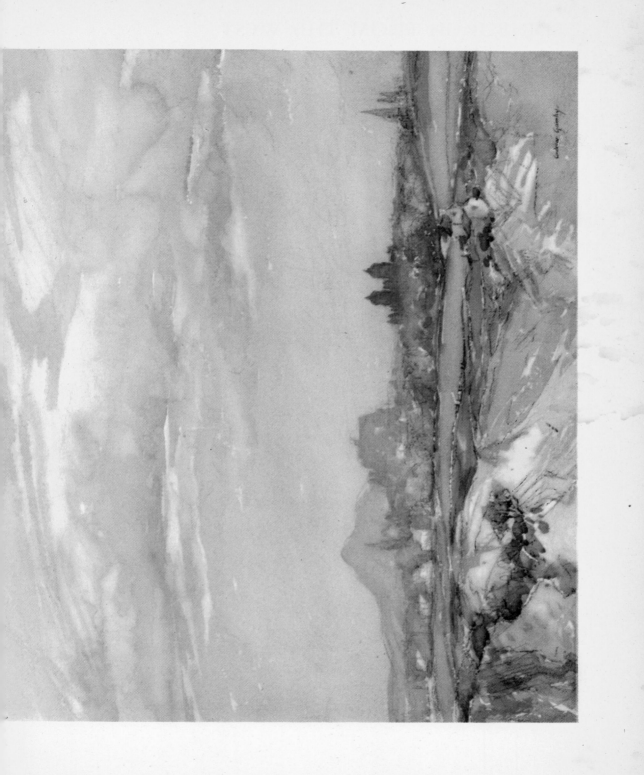

HOLYROOD PALACE

Alexander Zyw

Here Mary danced;
  Here Rizzio played;
Here rides Scotland's
  Cavalcade
In dust and dreams
  Around dead towers
Unwarmed by sunshine
  Unplashed by showers.

'The wisest fool'
  Moves shambling here
With Jinglin' Geordie
  At his ear;
And the last James
  Is setting off
For the Leith Links
  To play the 'goff'.

Charlie has left
  The lichtsome dance
To take the war
  At Prestonpans.
Laughter and sorrow
  Joy and tears
Mingle adown
  The dusty years.

Scots bairns we be
  Of every age;
Our bairn's delight
  To turn the page,
And at each coloured
  Picture look
In this old tattered
  Story-book.

EDINBURGH FROM CALTON HILL

Robert C. Robertson

Someone has already written the last word on this view, a little wider than what we see in this picture. Robert Louis Stevenson put it all down in his *Picturesque Notes*. He wrote:

'Of all places for a view, this Calton Hill is perhaps the best; since you can see the Castle which you lose from the Castle, and Arthur's Seat, which you cannot see from Arthur's Seat. . . . Immediately underneath upon the south, you command the yards of the High School, and the towers and courts of the new jail [now the Scottish Office]—a large place, castellated to the extent of folly, standing by itself on the edge of a steep cliff, and often joyfully hailed by tourists as the Castle. . . . From the bottom of the valley, a gigantic chimney rises almost to the level of the eye, a taller and a shapelier edifice than Nelson's Monument. Look a little farther, and there is Holyrood Palace, with its Gothic frontal and ruined abbey, and the red sentry pacing smartly to and fro before the door like a mechanical figure in a panorama. By way of an outpost, you can single out the little peak-roofed lodge, over which Rizzio's murderers made their escape and where Queen Mary herself, according to gossip, bathed in white wine to entertain her loveliness. Behind and overhead, lie the Queen's Park, from Muschat's Cairn to Dumbie-dykes, St. Margaret's Loch, and the long wall of Salisbury Crags: and thence, by knoll and rocky bulwark and precipitous slope, the eye rises to the top of Arthur's Seat, a hill for magnitude, a mountain in virtue of its bold design. This upon your left. Upon the right, the roofs and spires of the Old Town climb one above another to where the citadel prints its broad bulk and jagged crown of bastions on the western sky. Perhaps it is now one in the afternoon; and at the same instant of time, a ball rises to the summit of Nelson's flagstaff close at hand, and, far way, a puff of smoke followed by a report bursts from the half-moon battery at the Castle. This is the time-gun by which people set their watches, as far as the sea coast or in hill farms upon the Pentlands. . . . To complete the view, the eye enfilades Princes Street, black with traffic, and has a broad look over the valley between the Old Town and the New: here, full of railway trains and stepped over by the high North Bridge upon its many columns, and there, green with trees and gardens. . . . And while you are looking, across upon the Castle Hill, the drums and bugles begin to recall the scattered garrison; the air thrills with the sound; the bugles sing aloud; and the last rising flourish mounts and melts into the darkness like a star: a martial swan-song, fitly rounding in the labours of the day.'

THE FORTH BRIDGE

Robert C. Robertson

There is a hill in Fife, from the top of which on a clear day you can see the two great railway bridges which span the estuaries of Forth and Tay. In the distance the Tay Bridge is not impressive. "Like a sma' teeth comb', it was once described. But the Forth Bridge, in changing atmospheres, suggests now a web woven by some gigantic spider, now a boy's Meccano dream, now some strange Martian invasion formed in the brain of an H. G. Wells. So much for figures of speech. Now for figures of fact, and facts. The Forth and Tay Bridges have certain things in common. The first Tay Bridge was designed by Sir Thomas Bouch, and when it was being constructed in 1873, the Railway Companies asked Bouch to design a bridge over the Forth. Preparations for the building of that bridge—on the site of the present one—had advanced considerably (a brick pier on Inchgarvie had actually been built), when came that tragic Sunday of 28th December 1879, on which the first Tay Bridge fell. The result was that the whole construction of the Forth Bridge had to be reconsidered, and in 1883 Messrs Tancred, Arrol & Co. contracted to build a bridge to new designs by Sir John Fowler and Sir Benjamin Baker. In 1883 the work was begun. The cantilever, or the double-bracket, principle was adopted. And so to the figures. The total length of the bridge is 8,295 feet 9 inches (*i.e.*, just over one and a half miles). Excluding the viaduct approaches, the length is almost exactly one mile. The two main spans are each one-third of a mile. The rails are carried at a height of 157 feet above high water. The three central towers are 358 feet in height. Over 50,000 tons of steel were used in the construction, and 8,000,000 rivets hold the bridge together. Originally 250 tons of paint, and 35,000 gallons of oil were required for painting. Seven years were taken to the building and the cost was 3,500,000 pounds sterling. Between 4,000 and 5,000 men were employed on the work, and 57 lives were lost by accident. King Edward VII (then Prince of Wales) drove home the last rivet on March 4th, 1890.

The Forth Bridge

LADY STAIR'S HOUSE

Robert C. Robertson

This house in Lady Stair's Close, which was restored in 1913 by the then Lord Rosebery, is named after the wife of the first Earl of Stair, the man to whom is given the responsibility for the Massacre of Glencoe. But the lady, whose romance enshrouds the building, was the daughter of the first Earl of Loudoun, and wife in turn of Viscount Primrose, and John, second Earl of Stair. That lady has suffered much from legend, and her real story was excellently told by Miss Rosaline Masson in her *Edinburgh*. Miss Masson wrote:

'The story of that first marriage was adapted by Scott to form the plot of *Aunt Margaret's Mirror*. But Scott never knew the end of the romance; and, until some twenty years ago when a marriage entry was discovered in the registers of St. Peter's-upon-Cornhill, a scandal hung over the fair fame of Eleanor, Lady Stair. Kirkpatrick Sharpe, twenty years after her death, had told it to Robert Chambers, who included it in his *Traditions of Edinburgh*. The gossip of her time was that Lady Primrose, after the misery of her first marriage, vowed never to marry again, and that the infatuated Earl of Stair bribed her servants to admit him into her house, where, by appearing in his dressing-gown at the window of her oratory, he so scandalised the passers-by that the beautiful widow was forced to marry him to save her reputation. Nothing is said about this. But the entry in the Register, discovered two hundred years after, proves that the Earl in the oratory had been married to the widow of Lord Primrose six years before that event. Why were they married by licence, far from home, with concealment of titles? And why was their marriage kept secret in spite of the scandal? The reason was fully explained by a further discovery, this time in the Register House, Edinburgh, of the profligate Lord Primrose's will, which left the four children, three sons and a daughter, all under five years of age, to the care and guardianship of their mother—but only for as long as she remained unmarried. After that, they were to be taken from her and handed over to a cousin.

'Lord Stair died in 1747, forty years after that secret marriage at St. Peter's-upon-Cornhill. Lady Stair survived him for twelve years, living in Lady Stair's Close, with the only surviving one of her four children, the unmarried daughter, "Mistress Primrose". Long one of the queens of Edinburgh society, Lady Stair in her old age was noted and much envied for that luxury, a black servant—the only one in Edinburgh.'

Robert C. Robertson

NOVEMBER DAY, GEORGE STREET

Alan Ian Ronald

Perhaps a November day provides the proper atmosphere for George Street, which has turned its dignified back on what a student-editor once called 'the Peril and Pity of the Princes Street Parade', and in its austerity has selected to look north across grey waters to the hills. It is a reserved street with its banks and its churches, its statues and its monuments, its colonnades and its squares It has a certain serenity, only fitfully disturbed by the traffic which climbs up from Princes Street, hurries across it, and dives down the hill. In fact it is the kind of street, the past of which might re-live itself at any moment. There is no reason why the one Dundas should not come down from his monument and graciously greet that other Dundas emerging from the bank that was once his house, why John, Earl of Hopetoun, should not mount his monumental charger, and, as he rides along, salute the Prince Consort; there Robert Burns is on his way to Creech at No. 5, or to the Ferriers at No. 25; here is Walter Scott with his young bride on his arm making his way to their first home at No. 108, or again he is crossing to the Assembly Rooms where is being held that banquet at which the Unknown is to admit publicly his authorship of the Waverley Novels; they are writing for the *Review*, Sidney Smith at No. 46 and Jeffrey at No. 92; that noise of talking comes from No. 45, where Maga's mighty men have gathered; there from St. Andrew's Church comes the procession of the ministers of the Disruption on their way to Tanfield. But the dignified street has seen light-hearted spirits, too. Cockburn has left it on record how Professor Playfair, the Rev. Sidney Smith, and Thomas Thomson adventured greatly at the shop of a chemist, by name Gardiner, next door to the Assembly Rooms. 'Over the door was a head of the Greek doctor (was he a Greek?) which certain of our more intellectual members (the Friday Club) had long felt an itch to possess. However, one night, Playfair, Thomas Thomson, and Sidney Smith could resist no longer; they mounted the iron railing, and one of them got on the back of another, and had almost reached the prize, when Brougham, who had eagerly encouraged them to the exploit but had retired, was detected in the dim distance of the oil lamps, stealing up with the watch, for which he had wickedly gone. The assailants had just time to escape, and the guilded philosopher smiles a gracious defiance at this day.'

THE OLD DEAN BRIDGE

A. Bruce Thomson

While engaged in writing the descriptions of the pictures in this volume, I have found that one of my most constant companions has been David Balfour of Shaws. He has even accompanied me to the offices of the publishers in Tweeddale Court, for there he was, emerging from those offices (in his time the premises of the British Linen Company), a porter attending him with a bag of money. And so he comes with me by Lang Dykes (we call that highway Princes Street now) to 'the village of Dean, where it sits in a bottom of the glen beside the river . . . up the hill upon the further side by a plain path, and so to a decent-like small house in a garden of lawns and apple-trees'. We'll leave David at the garden-gate with Catriona taking his hand and kissing it, and telling him that 'the heart goes with the lips', and make our way about this little village left as a kind of something forgotten when Provost Learmonth engaged Telford to build his mighty bridge across the little Water of Leith, so that the Provost's lands on the north side might be tied to the great city. And while the greater Edinburgh grew and flourished on the north side of the water, the little Village of Dean was left alone to sleep and dream with its Baxter's crests, its crow-stepped gables, its trees and its mill, which, though now they grind in it sawdust for linoleum, is in direct historic succession to the flour-mills the wheels of which turned here centuries ago. Dean House, the home of the Nisbets, is remembered only by some of its stones, built into the walls of the cemetery which occupies its site, and which is the last resting-place of so many of Edinburgh's distinguished citizens. Here lie that famous author of *The Lays of the Scottish Cavaliers*, that famous surgeon Goodsir, that famous inventor Nasmyth, that famous judge Cockburn, that famous artist Sam Bough, and a host of others. A tale that is told, indeed, and the saddest epitaph that written by Alexander Nisbet, who published his *System of Heraldry* in 1772, and who told of the passing of the Nisbets of Dean (now all gone), how they were 'the only family of that name in Scotland that has the right, by consent, to represent the old original family of the name of Nisbet, since the only lineal male representer, the author of this system, is likely to go soon off the world, being an old man, and without issue male or female'.

OLD PLAYHOUSE CLOSE

Robert C. Robertson

> Can I contemplate on those dreary scenes
> Of mouldering desolation, and forbid
> The voice elegiac, and the falling tear!
> No more, from box to box, the basket, piled
> With oranges as radiant as the spheres,
> Shall with their luscious virtues charm the sense
> Of taste and smell. No more the gaudy beau
> With handkerchief in lavender well drenched,
> Or *bergamot*, or *rose-watero* pure,
> With flavoriferous sweets shall chase away
> The pestilential fumes of vulgar cits,
> Who, in impatience for the curtain's rise,
> Amused the lingering moments, and applied
> Thirst-quenching porter to their parched lips.

So wrote Robert Fergusson of 'The Canongate Playhouse in Ruins'. Although this Playhouse was the first theatre in Edinburgh to have the cachet of Royal Letters Patent, there had been many earlier 'stages' in the capital. Margaret Tudor had an official 'producer' in her train when she came up from England to marry our fourth James, and in the tennis court of Holyrood Palace that producer's cast staged *Interludes*. We would all like to believe that Shakespeare was 'on tour' with Lawrence Fletcher's company when they visited Edinburgh in 1599 and 1601, and played to packed houses in a theatre constructed by the King's command in Blackfriars Wynd. The Kirk did not approve, but James VI paid no attention to the strictures. Alan Ramsay opened a theatre in Carrubber's Close, but it was closed by Act of Parliament. Producers partially side-stepped that Act by opening halls for 'Concerts of Music', and by giving gratis performances of *Hamlet* and other plays in them. The theatre in Playhouse Close was at first designated 'New Concert Hall in the Canongate', and here the elder Sheridan played. Here also in December 1756, was produced Home's *Douglas*; but it was eleven years later before a proper theatre licence was obtained for this 'house' under Royal Letters Patent.

Mr. David Ross, the then manager, was a man of ideas, and he built a new theatre on the ground where the General Post Office now stands. It was on the stage of that theatre that Kemble and Mrs. Siddons played, with Walter Scott an enthusiastic member of the audience. On Mr. Ross's departure from the Canongate, the Playhouse fell into ruins.

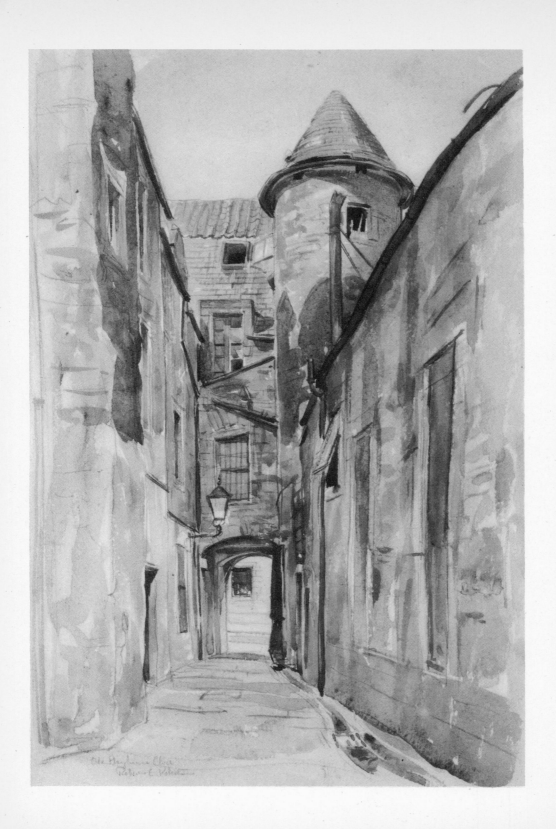

Old Bughanan Close
Robert C. Robertson

RIDDELL'S COURT, LAWNMARKET

Mrs. Cameron Kay

There's a quiet company of literary folk who rest in the Calton Cemetery. William Blackwood and Archibald Constable are there, all their publishing rivalry done. John Brown lies beside them with his dreams of Rab and Pet Marjorie. William Nicol takes his leisure there, all his Highland wanderings with Burns at an end, and there also David Hume at last found a place in Edinburgh from which he need make no change. For Hume was the most restless of dwellers in this city. He had many homes in Auld Reekie, but at Riddell's Court he found his first. Here he came in 1751, removing 'from the country to the town, the true scene for a man of letters'. While he dwelt here he was appointed Librarian to the Advocates' Library, and it was in this lodging that he began his *History of England*. But it is the ghost of a decent bailie body that is chief haunter of this Close. Macmoran was his name, and he was a wealthy merchant, a contemporary of George Heriot. In this court Macmoran lived and had his business, and twice in the year 1598 James VI came to dine in the bailie's fine old house, bringing with him his Queen, Anne of Denmark. In Macmoran's time the High School of Edinburgh occupied a position in the grounds of the Monastery of the Blackfriars, and the building backed on the Lawnmarket. The pupils of that period, being enraged at the cutting short of their holidays, barricaded themselves in the school, and refused to come out until the City Fathers granted them their proper vacation. Good Bailie John Macmoran collected some of the town's officers and marched on the school. He gave orders to break in the door, when one of the boys discharged a pistol, and shot the bailie dead. It was well for that lad that he was the son of Sinclair, Chancellor of Caithness. His blood saved his blood, and he became Sir William Sinclair of Mey.

But among all the ghosts that wander here, the kindliest surely is that of Patrick Geddes, who did so much to keep this court 'alive'.

THE SHRINE, SCOTTISH NATIONAL WAR MEMORIAL, EDINBURGH CASTLE

Robert C. Robertson

As a soldier of 'a working day', it is something to have had the experience of being in barracks in Edinburgh Castle during a period of the 1914–18 War. We were packed in then into every odd hole and corner, and troops filled all available quarters in Crown Square. Memory for us was busy about those places, for we were allowed to give a ball in the Banqueting Hall, which helped us to join up with all the history of the building on that south edge of the square. Then, with the passing of the years, they converted the building on the west side into a Naval and Military Museum, and that joined us up with all the nigh two-century-old story of our regiment. The east-side building was always thick with history. In it 'the wisest fool in Christendom' had been born; in it were the Crown Jewels. The old barrack on the north side—'Billings Building' they called it—was to become the most memorable place of all for us, for here they built the Scottish National War Memorial, which was dedicated on July 14th, 1927, and above the keystone of the central arch of the building, you can read the deeply carved words:

'To the Glory of God,
And in Memory of Scots who Fell, 1914–18.'

There is not space here to describe all the awe-inspiring stones that are built into this memorial. We can but say something of that part of it limned by Mr. Robertson in his picture 'The Shrine'. You see the iron gates as you gaze from the main doorway across the Hall of Honour, and poised in the stone arch beyond them is the figure of St. Michael, the Leader of the Hosts of Heaven. But the eyes are quickly focused on and held by the Stone of Remembrance, and its crown, the Casket. A piece of living rock protrudes through the paving, and bears upon its breast the stone with its Cross of Remembrance, cut into its green marble along with the words, 'Their Name Liveth'. Above it the Casket of Steel, with its guardian angels, holds the Rolls of Honour on which are written the names of our dear dead. A rich light falls upon it from the windows with their coloured symbolism, beginning with the Strife that slew Abel, and ending in the Sacrifice that saved the World. And then the eye comes to rest on the bronze frieze where are carved in relief figures representing one hundred typical warriors of that working day—and the memory of one comes back to you, and you go to your regiment's niche in the Hall of Honour, and open the book, and read the name, and for a little you are privileged to forget the withering and condemning of the years and what they have done to you, and you are young with them again at the going down of suns long set and in mornings long passed away.

THE WEST BOW

James Miller

In his *Old Edinburgh*, 1939, Mr. Ian G. Lindsay makes the following plea:

'If Edinburgh is to maintain her dignity and her beauty, to remain an ancient city in more than mere repute, the fine houses of the Old Town must be preserved as living homes for her people. Nearly all those listed can be reconditioned for housing, a fact already proved in several reconstructions by the city authorities. These old houses *are* Edinburgh's history: the outward form of history, more expressive than any written word. With their stately proportions, their gablets and dormers, their crow-steps, their pends and wynds, and the moulded stones and carved inscriptions in their walls, they have a beauty and charm that provide for many of us the essential picture of our city.'

Mr. Lindsay lists all the houses seen in the painting. The corner house is dated 1561. Mr. Lindsay makes particular mention of the second house from the right of the picture. He writes:

'89 West Bow. House with crow-stepped gable facing the street. There are string courses beneath the windows on each floor, and below the apex of the gable, front and back, are two pigeon entrances with an alighting ledge. This and the preceding houses stand next one another and form one of the best groups of old street architecture in Scotland. Their preservation as a whole should be assured before it is too late.'

It is interesting to compare Mr. Lindsay's view with that of Mr. Daniel Wilson writing just one hundred years ago:

'In the centre of the ancient city there stood, till a few years since, a strange, crooked, steep, and altogether singular and picturesque avenue from the High Street to the low valley on the south, in which the more ancient extensions of the once circumscribed Scottish capital are reared. Scarcely anything can be conceived more curious and whimsically grotesque than its array of irregular stone gables and timber galleries, that seemed as if jostling one another for room along the steep and narrow thoroughfare. The modern visitor who now sees the "Bow-head", an open area nearly on a level with the Castle draw-bridge, and then by gradual and easy descent of long flights of stairs, and the more gentle modern slope of Victoria Street, at length reaches "The Bowfoot Well" in the Grassmarket, will hardly be persuaded that between these two widely different elevations there extended only a few years since a thoroughfare crowded with antique tenements, quaint inscriptions, and still more strange and interesting associations; unmatched in its historic and traditionary memories by any other spot of the curious old capital, whose memories we seek to revive.'

It would appear that in this preservation it has always been too late.

The West Bow, Edinburgh. 1924

FIFE

Artists

A. S. BLACK

STEWART CARMICHAEL

ANNA DIXON

DAVID FOGGIE

KEITH HENDERSON

M. V. MACGEORGE

JAMES MILLER

R. B. NISBET

ALEXANDER N. PATERSON

S. J. PEPLOE

ALAN IAN RONALD

JOHN G. SPENCE SMITH

G. P. H. WATSON

JAMES WRIGHT

THE CASTLE OF ST. ANDREWS

M. V. MacGeorge

The strange flock of migrants in their brilliant plumage—the summer visitors—have gone; the Autumn Meeting of the Royal and Ancient Golf Club is over, and the Captains and the kings of golf have departed. A benign peace has settled over the old grey city of St. Andrews. Nature provides her kindly days and nights of purification—the days of clear light and long vistas across the green of the links to the Angus hills, cut sharp like cardboard scenery against great banks of cumulus, and over the grey-blue bay, where far out on the waters of the North Sea the Bell Rock Lighthouse stands like a white candle in a bowl of Copenhagen ware. The light and the sharp cold and the wind seem to act as an elixir on the old town, which becomes fresh and young and vigorous again in those pleasant day-times, and falls to a quiet sleep as the gold of a far sunset fades to dove-grey, and the air is filled with the crying and the faint shadows of the moving wings of wild geese.

And so this clear October morning light smiles on a young vigorous Alma Mater of a city, whose children gather around her knee. There is something of fairy-tale about the sudden flash of a red gown in a grey street, then the flash of another, and then a surging of red gowns, where there are good shouting and good laughter, and hope and happiness, as if out of the hill the children had all come back to Hamelin Town. But the hills from which they come are many and wide-spread across all the world.

The castle grounds are splashed with red, but the red is not the blood that has been shed about those walls, but the scarlet of the gowns of students at their books in a place of peace.

Seven hundred and fifty years! Such is the castle's age. Edward, the Hammer, was here; twice the English held it, but Wallace's Sir Andrew Moray drove them out, and destroyed the castle. Rebuilt, it was a schoolroom for James I (schoolmaster Wardlaw), for James II (schoolmaster Kennedy). It has been Archbishop's Palace, and Martyr's prison. It saw Wishart and Beaton, each murdered. John Knox dispensed the Lord's Supper in it. By 1655 it was a ruin. Perhaps it likes best to remember that in its heyday, as now in its ruins, it acted and acts as a schoolroom for scholars.

CERES, FIFE

S. J. Peploe

The village green of Ceres has a long story. Here, they say, the men of the district collected and marched over the Old Bridge on their way to Bannockburn; and to see Ceres aright to-day you must come to that green, when the Fife Foxhounds have a meet there, or on the local market-day, when young men express their affection for fair maidens in gifts of 'sugar herts', and when they race ponies with bookies and betting an' a'. But if you'll come wandering around the village with me now, we can have a look at the old Weigh-House, at the entrance to which are a pair of jougs, and a carving of scales, where weights are on one side, and a bale on the other, and above which we read 'God bless the just'. In the parish kirk we will find an effigy of a knight in armour who was laid to rest some time in the fourteen hundreds, and north-east of the church, in a twelfth-century vault, members of the Lindsay family are sleeping. Built into an old garden wall we will find a seventeenth-century double fireplace, on which horsemen are galloping, footmen are marching, and a piper is playing. In it, at a later date, has been inserted a panel on which is carved a Toby Jug. That Toby is known as The Provost, for so it has been named by its maker in letters of stone.

But while we are here, I think you might care to walk up the hill to Scotstarvit Tower, and listen across three centuries to the laughter of Sir John Scot, who had Timothy Pont's maps engraved and printed in Amsterdam, and who made the collection of Latin poems by Scottish writers, known as *Delitiæ Poetarum Scotorum*. Sir John's laughter mingles with that of his brother-in-law, William Drummond of Hawthornden, and his wife, Lady Scot, for they are reading bits from the *Polemo-Middinia*, the first macaronic poem published in Scotland. The poem was their own work, and is supposed to describe in its quaint mixture of Scots and dog-Latin a dispute between Lady Scot (Drummond's sister) and Lady Cunninghame of the Barns (Drummond's sweetheart). You might also care to laugh at this short excerpt:

> Nymphae, quae colitis highissima monta Fifaea,
> Seu vos Pittenwema tenent, seu Crelia crofta,
> Sive Anstraea domus, ubi nat haddocus in undis,
> Codlineusque ingens, et fleucca et sketta pererrant
> Per costam, et scopulis lobster monifootus in udis
> Creepat, et in mediis ludit whitenius undis.

BALMERINO ABBEY

Stewart Carmichael

I always find myself in the company of two grey kindly ghosts when I visit the Abbey of Balmerino which lies open to the sun on the south bank of the estuary of the River Tay.   When I come on the abbey from the north I meet them, working amid the ghosts of plum trees in the field next the ruins, for that field was the plum yard, and there in the days of their flesh laboured Thomas Stevinson and John Yester (*ultimi Romanorum* they termed themselves), two old monks who were all that were left of the convent. Yester slipped away, and Stevinson was left alone in the year 1600.   He had been a monk in the abbey since before 1535—and had seen all the glory pass away.

And a great glory had this Benedictine abbey been! Here was holy ground as far back as we can go, for a companion of St. Regulus of the legend, Saint Mernach, had his 'bal' here. Local folk to this day call the place 'Balmirny'. Margaret, Canmore's Queen, was the influence behind the idea of the foundation, and in the last month of the year 1229, William the Lion's widow, the good Queen Ermengarde, with the full approval of her son, Alexander II, placed a convent of twelve Melrose monks here. Here four years later, when her pilgrimage was over, they buried Ermengarde. Queens are closely connected with this abbey, for an abbot accompanied Margaret, Alexander's daughter, to 'Norroway' to see her wed to King Eric, and that abbot is one of the 'Scots lords' who lie at the feet of Sir Patrick Spens where

> Half ower, half ower to Aberdour
> 'Tis fifty fathoms deep.

The fourth of the fair ladies was James V's Queen for a day, the Princess Madeleine of France. Poor lass, she was so frail, she could not ride on horseback, and the Edinburgh fogs were her sore enemies. So the King chose for her the 'Abbacie of Balmerinoch, as having the best aers of any places in the Kingdom, for her residence and abode'. But we cannot be certain whether she came or not. It is perhaps unlikely, for forty-nine days after she landed in Scotland, she was dead.

In 1547 Sir Thomas Wyndham, the English pillager of Edinburgh, burned the abbey. It was rebuilt in time for the fifth Queen's visit, for here Mary, Queen of Scots, spent some two days in 1565, on her way to St. Andrews, where she was to have the happiest hours of her life. Then the abbey died for ever of the lingering fever of the Reformation.

So, as we leave this place in the gloaming, the grey ghost of Brother Stevinson moves among the ghosts of the plum trees, remembering the ghosts.

BARKING NETS, PITTENWEEM

David Foggie

I am glad that in the picture-book, which is personal memory, I can still see an east-coast Scottish fishing-fleet making harbour—no auxiliary engines, no steam of any kind, just the dark-brown sails, proud and gallant, above the white line on the very edge of the boat, and beneath the broad band of red, blue, or green above the black of the hull; and can still read again the names painted on the prows: fisher-lasses' names like *Annie Cargill*; some not so definite like *Bonnie Lass*; names of personal quality like *Endeavour*; a whole galaxy of *Stars*; sometimes a Latin name; sometimes a French one; and sometimes a hope expressed as in *Providence*. The boats were 'fifies' mostly, one of the three famous classes of Scots fishing-craft. The other two types were the 'scaffie' and the 'zulu'. They were all double-ended luggers. The 'scaffies' were the earliest form. They were modelled on Norse boats, and were not decked. They were originally built in Buckie, and were three-masted, each mast carrying a lug sail. A later variety had only two masts, each of which could be lowered, and was decked. The 'fifies' were more powerful boats, and the larger ones were fully decked. The first 'zulu' was constructed by William Campbell, of Lossiemouth, whose 'fifie forward and scaffie aft' boat, *None Such*, took the water in 1879. In his *Fishermen and Fishing Ways*, Mr. Peter Anson gives the following details of one traditional story of the building of the 'zulu'. He writes:

'A young Lossiemouth fisherman had married a Buckie girl, and they wanted to build a new boat. The husband, who had always sailed in a boat of the Fifie class, naturally wanted to build one after this model, but the wife's father owned a Skaffie, and she obstinately stuck out for the latter type, especially as she was defraying half the cost. After much discussion and argument a compromise was finally arrived at: the husband got his way as regards the bow, while the wife won as to the lines of the stern, and that, so they say, is the origin of the first Zulu.'

In a volume showing pictures recording Scottish buildings of interest, which might have suffered by the war, it is not out of place to give a picture which shows one class of guardians of those buildings in war-time, guardians, many of whom were obliterated by the war. The Scots fisherman held one of our most dangerous front-lines in the war, the front-line we can never afford to lose.

CRAIGHALL, CERES, FIFE

Keith Henderson

The great stone eagle with a leveret in its claws broods over the ruin it has made of a life, as Time seems to sit here and brood over the ruins of this strange French Renaissance-Italian façade grafted on to an older building, taking a grim pleasure in the motto in the pediment, 'Spero Suspiro Donec' (While I breathe, I hope), placed there by one of those Hope judges, who looked after the law in the days of James VI, his sons and grandsons. The first Hope bought the property from a David Kinnimond who made a practice of quarrelling with Thomas Buchanan, the parson of Ceres, and being bound over to keep the peace. This Buchanan was a nephew of the great George, and was at one time a Regent in St. Salvator's College, St. Andrews. Lord Advocate Hope, the new owner, was a descendant of a French nobleman, who had come over in the time of Magdalen of France. Tradition has it that in some earlier building on this spot dwelt Michael Scot, the Wizard.

The most interesting part of the ruins is not shown in this picture. It is the entrance gate which is mid-sixteenth century, and is part of the farm buildings, behind which stand the stones depicted for us by Mr. Henderson. On the right hand is seen the old building with a stair-tower, which contained the main entrance. Along with other older parts of the castle this stair-tower is rubble-built. The florid part of the building has a date 1697, and it is supposed to have been designed by Sir William Bruce.

The arches in this façade were apparently never filled with glass, so that the possibility is that the rooms were actually further back, and that those arches acted as a front to some kind of balcony.

CROSS WYND, FALKLAND

Anna Dixon

I do not know who Nicholas Moncrief was, but opposite to the entrance to Falkland Palace the house he built in 1610 still stands, with his initials over the doorway. All we know of his lady is that her initials were A. O. Another panel tells us that James VI gave Nicholas this land, for which Nicholas expressed himself as truly thankful. Many other of those old houses in Falkland saw James riding in those twisted streets of which Cross Wynd is one. Rotten Row is another. Names like Parliament Square, College Close, and West Port, suggest a one-time vigorous life in this old-time town, which became a Royal Burgh as early as 1458, and which had four annual fairs. The only thing in those early times that appears not to have been up to standard in this ancient burgh was its ale. For Sir David Lindsay in his 'Testament and Complaynt of the Papyngo' writes of it thus:

> Fair weill, Falkland! the fortrace of Fyfe,
> Thy polyte park, under the Lowmound Law!
> Sum tyme in thee, I led ane lusty lyfe,
> The fallow deir to see thame raik on raw.
> Court men to cum to thee, thay stand grait aw,
> Sayand, thy burgh bene, of all burrowis, baill,
> Because, in thee, thay never gat gude aill.

In another of those old Falkland houses there was born about the year 1648 Richard Cameron, who matriculated at the University of St. Andrews in 1662, and graduated in 1665. He came under the influence of the field-preachers, crossed over to Holland, but returned to Scotland in 1680 to become himself a field-preacher. Along with another St. Andrews student, Cargill, at Sanquhar he revoked allegiance to Charles II, declared war against him, and formed the Cameronian Regiment (now 1st Scottish Rifles). Cameron was killed at Airdsmoss.

48

DUNFERMLINE ABBEY

Stewart Carmichael

It is some thirty-five years now since MacGregor Chalmers discovered, beneath the nave of the present Abbey of Dunfermline, traces of the foundations of that first church built by Malcolm Canmore's Queen. The outline of that building has since been traced on the floor of the nave, and gratings have been let into the floor at certain points so that the pious observer may view parts of the original founds. David I commenced building his great monastic church here in 1128, but nothing is left of it now except the nave, which has been described as 'one of the finest surviving examples of Scots-Norman monastic architecture'. The church was greatly extended in the thirteenth century, a special addition being the Chapel of St. Margaret. Each century has seen some further change on the great building. In the fourteenth the choir was enlarged, and many windows changed from Romanesque to Gothic; in the fifteenth the north-west tower was rebuilt; in the sixteenth the tower had added to it the present bartizan and spire; in the seventeenth many of the aisles were strengthened by buttresses; in the nineteenth the south-west tower was restored and the present parish church built. Queen Margaret and her husband were buried in the ruined chapel at the east end of the church. The early conventual buildings were completely destroyed by Edward I, but were rebuilt during the fourteenth century. Later the guest-house was substantially increased in size, and became a royal palace. James V, his daughter Mary, and his grandson James, resided on occasion in that palace, and Charles II was the last monarch to use it. In the year 1708 the roof collapsed, and that was the end of another 'auld sang'.

FALKLAND PALACE

G. P. H. Watson

There is a tale of this old Fifeshire palace which rivals Dumas' story of the Duke of Buckingham and Anne of Austria's diamond studs. In the Falkland incident it was another Queen Anne, this time of Denmark, and her husband was King James the Sixth, sub-titled so many things, from 'God's silly vassal' to 'the wisest fool in Christendom'. So to a summer's day in the 'garden yearde', and another fool, Alexander Ruthven, sleeping in the sun. King James, walking in the garden, has his eye caught by a ribbon round Alexander's neck—and James recognizes the ribbon as one given by him to the Queen. Then 'this walking pathological museum' of a King went off 'spitting, hawking, and blowing his nose' to find out all about it. But a Scottish Madame Bonacieux is on the watch, removes the ribbon from Ruthven's neck, speeds to the Queen's boudoir, and, when the puffing, panting James arrives, to ask concerning his gift, a smiling Queen produces it—and James can only gape.

It is something to have a tale of laughter—even if it be apocryphal—about Falkland Palace. For here are tears enow. The *Scotichronicon* tells us that in 1337 English soldiers burned the first 'Tower of Falkland' to the ground. In its successor the poor Duke of Rothesay died. It was James II who began the extensions which converted the 'tower' into a 'castle', but James IV was the King who made a 'palace' out of it as a kind of bridal gift to his Queen, Margaret Tudor. His son, James V, made further additions as a kind of bridal gift to his Queen, Magdalen of France, and added to it still further when he married Mary of Guise. It was in this palace, that, when he lay dying, they brought news to him of the birth of Mary, who was to be Queen of Scots, and 'it cam wi' a lass and 'twill gang wi' a lass', the King is said to have prophesied. 'He spak litle from then forth, bot turned his bak to his lordis and his face to the wall'.

Mary spent some time in Falkland, as did James VI, but, once London turned the latter into an Anglo-Scot, Falkland ceased to interest the Royal Family. Charles I and Charles II each visited the Palace, but that was the end. Cromwell's soldiers made a mess of it, and gradually the whole edifice fell into ruin. In the second half of the nineteenth century the south wing of the building and the gate-house were restored. Perhaps the most interesting structure is the old-time tennis-court, which is, as far as I know, the only one of its kind in Scotland.

FERNIE CASTLE, FIFE

Keith Henderson

Fernie Castle is an instance of the very good blend of the old and the new. The western end is all that remains of the original sixteenth-century building—a square type of keep, looking down on a courtyard, over which the modern part of the house has been built. The newelled stair still remains in the tower, but windows, etc., have all been modernized. There is a charter dated 5th March 1509–10, in which the King, who fell at Flodden, gives a man, with the strange name of Florentinus Adinulty, permission to build on the lands of Fernie 'a sufficient mansion of stone and lime, with hall, chambers, barns, byres, stables, dovecots, orchards, gardens and beehives; and also to plant oaks and other trees'. For many generations the Fernies of Fernie were Foresters of Falkland and Custodians of Cupar. In the Old Kirk of Cupar under a canopy bearing the arms of the Fernies of Fernie is the figure of a knight in armour.

OLD TENEMENTS, CULROSS

James Miller

The National Trust for Scotland are busy, at this time of writing, reconditioning old houses in Culross in such a way that those houses can supply the demands of modern life and yet retain their dignity and their personality. It is very pleasant to visit a castle or a dower-house where lives are lived in usefulness and pleasantness with the tradition continually present in, for example, portrait or piece of furniture of all the lives which have been lived within those same walls. There is no reason why lives should not be lived in usefulness and pleasantness in those humbler dwellings, where the place of the portraits and the furniture is taken by the worn treads of an outside stair which tell of all the lost footsteps. In many of our cities and towns renovations of such houses have taken place, and they are a matter of delight to the eye of the beholder, and satisfactory to the dwellers therein. Old stone walls and old roof-tiles have not merely an aesthetic value, they are proof against the wildest of our weather, and they engender a sense of quiet and peace and permanence, which are good things to have in those days. In Culross the reconditioning of old houses has a special merit, since in those houses will live folk who will carry on the life of the community in the way and from the angle of the folk who lived in those houses long ago. The historic tradition will be continued in all its best senses.

RED ROW, LIMEKILNS

Alan Ian Ronald

No kilns glow with the burning of lime in Limekilns to-day. We have to go back to the time of James V to see that industry in full swing here. There is one old house in the village, bearing the date 1581, and named 'The King's Cellar', which tradition says was the home of that distinguished Scotsman, Robert Pitcairn, who was first Commendator of Dunfermline.

But Limekilns owed its reputation more to fiction than to fact, or rather to fact localized in fiction by a master of the craft. One of the most entertaining diaries of the '45 is that of the Chevalier de Johnstone. He was aide-de-camp to Lord George Murray, and after Culloden made his way as a fugitive over the Grampians and down across Angus to Broughty Ferry. He was recommended to a Mrs. Burn who kept an inn in that village, and she put Johnstone in touch with two boatmen, who might ferry him across the Tay. But the boatmen were afraid of the Hanoverian Dragoons in the neighbourhood, and would not take the risk. Let the Chevalier now tell his story:

'I perceived that the two daughters of Mrs. Burn, who were as beautiful as Venus, were not objects of indifference to the boatmen, from the glances they bestowed upon them from time to time. I therefore quitted the stupid boatmen, and attached myself to these two pretty girls, with the view of gaining them over to my interest.

'In less than half an hour my two beauties were entirely in my interest, and each of them made a vigorous assault on her sweetheart, making use of all manner of prayers and entreaties, but with as little success as I had had. The beautiful and charming Mally Burn, the eldest of the two, said to her sister, "O, Jenny! they are despicable cowards and poltroons. I would not for the world that this unfortunate gentleman was taken in our house. I pity his situation. Will you take an oar? I shall take another, and we will row him over ourselves, to the eternal shame of these pitiful and heartless cowards." Jenny consented without hesitation.

'We left Broughty at ten o'clock in the evening, and reached the opposite shore of this arm of the sea, which is about two miles in breadth, near midnight. . . . My two beauties landed with me, to put me in the highway that leads to St. Andrews; and I took leave of them, deeply affected with their generous sentiments, and heroic courage.'

And so enter Robert Louis Stevenson, and the fact is turned into the most delightful fiction. Limekilns takes the place of Broughty, Alison Hastie the place of Mally Burn, and there go David Balfour and Alan Breck across the Forth. And as David and Alan stand on the south shore, and watch Alison pulling back across the waters, Alan says, 'It is a very fine lass, David, a very fine lass.'

ST. ANDREWS FROM THE EAST

R. B. Nisbet

She was green April in the street;
  October dark ghosted with darker towers.
Sunlight tree-filtered round her feet.
  Her mouth was cliff-top flowers.
    Winds drove wild hair across her quiet eyes
      When, on the midnight sands,
      Virgin she walked with benison
        In her long-fingered hands.

Her land the dunes that drank the light,
  And left thirst-quenching emptiness of dark;
Her waters dawn-grey sea all smothered white;
  Her song a morning lark.
    Now etched in silence all her city-cloud
      Lies in a mist of sea,
      Uncharted from the first of days
        To all eternity.

Nor shall her gates now open wide
  To this poor, broken, useless key of tears.
No weapon but is scattered dust beside
  The flaming sword of years.
    For there was never spring again
      Nor leaves atune with breeze,
      And no man heard a singing bird
        In man-lost Eden trees.

ST. MONANCE, LOOKING EAST

A. S. Black

In the winter gales the waters of the grey North Sea rush up and jump the dyke of the graveyard in St. Monance, as if trying to call back from their dead home in the earth the men who lived all their lives on the sea. The houses of the fisher-people crowd and crush together down the steep incline from the fields to the water as if they, too, were being held from their rightful place—the sea. The boats, also, in the packed harbour convey the impression of kennelled dogs, struggling to get rid of their chains and to be on the trail of their quarry—the herring. A prosperous little fishing-village this, and has been for many a day. The parish minister, who wrote about it for the *New Statistical Account*, tells us that (about 1790) 'for the wet, hungry, and weary fisherman, who has been at sea since two or three o'clock in the morning, there is a blazing fire, and a clean substantial breakfast set out, to which he sits down with much relish and enjoyment. The ordinary food of the people is oatmeal, potatoes and fish.'

And they build powerful and graceful boats at St. Monance, and I think of one so built lying in the harbour below me here, which carries parties of student-zoologists over to the Isle of May in the search for the clinical material they require.

Most occupations have their poets. The fishermen of St. Monance had theirs. He lies in an unmarked grave, in the lea of that churchyard dyke of which I have written. His name was Thomas Mather, and he was born in St. Monance in 1794. He went a'sailing in the brig *Gem* of Inverkeithing. He was ashore in Venice, when he was hailed by a gentleman, who conversed with him for some time of Scotland. That gentleman was another Scottish poet, George Gordon, Lord Byron: and Mather told the story a thousand times of how: 'The stranger pressed my hand when we parted. . . . I never saw a king but once, and it was he.'

One verse I quote from Mather's little volume, *Musings by Sea and Shore*:

> There's little pleasure in the hoose—
> There's nought but sulk and gloom,
> Then wae's me for the fisherman,
> That rows his boatie toom.

THE PENDS, DUNFERMLINE

James Wright

'Domus in qua fratres una comedunt in signum mutui amoris.' So the old monks described the 'Frater'—'the house in which the brethren eat together in token of mutual love'. We see the great west window of the Frater of Dunfermline Abbey in Mr. Wright's picture of 'The Pends'. The tracery at the top of the seven lights is of the type used in Canterbury. The projecting part of the building contains a turnpike stair, which is crowned by a cap-house and a spire. Above 'The Pends' (technically a vaulted transe) are the two storeys of the gate-house, and at the top of the second storey is the corbelling for a bartizan. This gate-house joined up the Frater with the kitchens of the palace. The present gate-house was constructed somewhere towards the end of the fourteenth century, but there are traces of an earlier building. The fact that all the conventual buildings of Dunfermline Abbey were destroyed by Edward I, recalls to mind that gate-house of the other Scottish abbey which in the fourteenth century rivalled Dunfermline—the Abbey of Aberbrothock. Edward I destroyed Dunfermline because it was a meeting-place for the Scottish barons in the War of Independence. So it was in the Regality Chamber in the Abbey of Aberbrothock, a chamber which is right above the Pends of that abbey, that those barons gathered to sign and forward to the Pope their letter declaring the Independence of Scotland. But it was in Dunfermline Abbey that Bruce was laid to rest by the side of his Queen. Writes Barbour:

> They haiff had him to Dunferlyne,
> And him solemnly yirded syne,
> In a fair tomb into the quire:
> Bishops and prelates that were there
> Assolizied him, when the service
> Was done, as they could best devise;
> And syne, upon the other day,
> Sorry and wo they went their way,
> And he debowelled was cleanly,
> And also balmed syne full richly;
> And the worthy Lord of Douglas,
> His heart, as it forspoken was,
> Received him in great dewtie,
> And fair and great solemnitie.

ST. ANDREWS CATHEDRAL

Alexander N. Paterson

'A long farewell to thee, sea-washed seat of holy Andrew, pleasant to me in life and ever greatly longed for; and now art thou ever dearer, little town, in that thou gavest me, out-worn, rest eternal after toil.'

In this place of sleep it is well to begin with an epitaph. The above is a translation from the Greek of Alexander Shewan, which is on the mural tablet in the Collegiate Church of St. Salvator to the memory of Andrew Lang. Lang is laid to rest in the shadow of the ruins of the Cathedral of St. Andrews, and 'within sound of the sea'.

Eight hundred years ago they laid the foundations of this place. Two hundred years it was in the building. Edward the Hammer stripped its roof, and it was not until 1318 that Bishop Lamberton re-consecrated it in the presence of his friend and King, Robert Bruce. A hundred years later Prior Haldenstone beautified it. In it James V married the Princess who was to be the mother of Queen Mary of Scots; in it were tried and condemned Patrick Hamilton, George Wishart and Walter Myln. Then neglect—not Knox—saw the decay of a great building. Charles I thought about restoring it—but got no further than the thought. The ruins became the town quarry, and a quarry indeed it was till less than a hundred and fifty years ago, when the debris was removed.

And just after that debris was removed, Sir Walter Scott came to the ruins here, and wrote:

'I sat down on a gravestone, and recollected the first visit I made to St. Andrews, now thirty-four years ago. I remembered the name I then carved in Runic characters on the turf beside the castle-gate, and I asked why it should still agitate my heart. But my friends came down from the tower, and the foolish idea was chased away.'

And Scott thought of the lines

And many a lad I loved is dead
And many a lass grown old,

which, my sorrow, are the lines in all men's hearts, who come back to a City of Youth.

So before we leave the cathedral of kings and queens, archbishops and priors, let us look at one epitaph to youth. There on part of the cathedral masonry is a monument, on which is carved in bas-relief, the three-quarter life-size figure of a golfer addressing his ball. It is a tribute to young Tom Morris, who died 25th December 1875 in the twenty-fifth year of his age, and as Shewan paid his tribute to Lang, so on this stone Principal Tulloch paid his tribute to Tommy:

DEEPLY REGRETTED BY NUMEROUS FRIENDS AND ALL GOLFERS HE THRICE IN SUCCESSION WON THE CHAMPION BELT AND HELD IT WITHOUT RIVALRY AND YET WITHOUT ENVY HIS MANY AMIABLE QUALITIES BEING NO LESS ACKNOWLEDGED THAN HIS GOLFING ACHIEVEMENTS

ST. MONANCE KIRK

John G. Spence Smith

He must have been a wild lad, Tam Aitone, and Beatrix Youlles, 'a gey lass' as they say in Fife, for on the nineteenth day of November in the year 1648 Tam was summoned by the Kirk Session of St. Monance for drinking and 'byding' in that lady's 'hous in time of sermon'.   Tam did not improve, for we read in the Records that he 'went by the Kirk door on the Lord's Day at the minister's going to the pulpitt, blowing and blasting tobacco, and came not to the kirk'.   Tam may have repented later, for you cannot imagine General David Leslie standing any nonsense from the likes of him; and two years after Tam's 'blasting', that famous soldier was made ruling elder of the Kirk of St. Monance, and in it thanksgivings were held later for his victories over Montrose.

From the sea or from the land this Parish Church of St. Monance can be beheld from afar, and the old approach to it has a quality all its own.   You will still find the cuttings in the rocks which mark the old way by the seashore, and which were made so that the path might be easier for worshippers.

Like all tales of our old kirks, that of St. Monance has its beginning in the dim mists of tradition with the Saint himself, a dweller in a cave here, cruelly murdered by the Danes.   There was some kind of chapel here long before King David II—somewhat nastily wounded by an arrow, and somewhat mistily saved with his Queen from shipwreck—founded this chapel 'anew'.   Under his instructions work was begun on the building in 1362, and they went as far afield as Inverness for the wood, and to a travelling guild for the masons.   About 1477 the chapel was acquired by the Dominican Friars, and they made of the place 'a hospice'.   Seventy years later the English burned it down, and one century afterwards it was turned into a parish kirk.   As such, however, it was not popular, and it was allowed to 'fall into a ruinous condition'.   In 1828 they set about a proper restoration, with William Burn, the designer of the renovation of the exterior of St. Giles', Edinburgh, as architect.

The church originally consisted of the choir, south and north transepts, and a square tower, but no nave as is also the case in such old religious foundations as Seton and Roslin. The high altar was at the east end, but Mr. Burn made his main entrance there, and closed the original west-end door, the position of which would suggest that the building was never meant to house a congregation, but to act merely as a chapel where a friar 'should daily offer up thanksgivings for the preservation of the founder'.

But if you come along that path on the rocks some dark night, and suddenly to your nostrils is blown the smell of strong tobacco, you need not worry.   It is but the kindly ghost of Tam Aitone 'blowing and blasting'.

THE STUDY, CULROSS

James Miller.

There are, I should imagine, very few buildings which are named after a room, but this happens in the case of that crow-stepped gabled house in the Forth-side Fifeshire village of Culross, known as the 'Study'. The actual 'study', which simply means a private room, is a small apartment at the very top of the house reached by a narrow turret-stair. Though 1633 is the date on the door of the house, the actual building may be some thirty years older. The 'Study' is now the property of The National Trust, and Mr. Robert Hurd, in his *Scotland Under Trust* (1939), describes it thus:

'The "Study" contains a wide circular stair to the second-floor above which is the small stair that occupies the corbelled turret seen from below. The main stair leads to two large rooms, one of which is partly lined with unusually refined oak panelling, some sections of inlaid panelling from the same room having been deposited several years ago in the Royal Scottish Museum, Edinburgh. One would like to see this returned to its original position. The windows on the road frontage of the "Study" have been renewed with the same leaded glazing and shutter-boards we have seen at the "Palace". The ground floor has been modernised as a dwelling with its own street entrance. Eventually the National Trust hopes to furnish the unoccupied partly panelled upper rooms of the "Study" with pieces of the period in order to give the public some idea of what these rooms looked like when they were used by their original occupants.'

The Market Cross in the foreground has a modern shaft inserted in its original octagonal four-stepped base.

Culross   James Miller 1942.

THE TOWN HALL, CRAIL

A. S. Black

> Next, from the well-aird town of Crail
> Go out her craftsmen with tumultuous din—
> Her wind-bleached fishers, sturdy-limb'd and hale,
> Her in-kneed tailors, garrulous and thin;
>
> And some are flushed with horns of pithy ale,
> And some are fierce with drains of smuggled gin,
> While, to augment his drouth, each to his jaws
> A good Crail capon holds, at which he rugs and gnaws.

So Tennant described the folk of this 'well-aird' Fife village hurrying on their way to see Maggie Lauder and Rab the Ranter at Anster Fair. The lower part of this Tolbooth Tower might have witnessed their departure along the coast road, for it was built in 1517. There is a curious capital and base of twelfth-century workmanship built into the south side probably stolen from the church. Those circular windows are only some two hundred years old. Built into the eastern, and relatively modern, part of the building is a panel bearing a ship flying a flag at the top of the mast, and a crescent moon and six stars. At the top is a date, which appears to read 1602, and the word, Crail, is carved underneath. A Dutch bell hangs in the steeple, the inscription on which tells how it was cast in 1520. The Parish Church of Crail, which lies further north on the other side of the same street as the Tolbooth, has portions of twelfth-century construction, and a tower of the early thirteenth. In the belfry hangs another Dutch bell, cast by Peter van den Ghein in 1614. In the street below that in which the Tolbooth is situated, there are some remains of a nunnery, the garden of which is still garden ground, and in that garden these verses were written:

> She wedded God, the slim, white lass
> That walked here long long years ago.
> In quiet thought she let them pass
> —The hours, soft-footed, gentle, slow,
> Shadows upon the fragrant grass.
>
> One day a wind from space of sea
> And laden with a flower's kiss
> Bore to her sense its witchery.
> The tears came blinding all her bliss,
> Tears for the world all cast away.
> How gladly had she changed that day
> A rose for all her rosary.
>
> A man walks here. The scent of flowers
>   Old hopes awaken,
> And he must weep his wealth of hours
>   The world has taken.

GLASGOW AND THE WEST

Artists

W. MARSHALL BROWN

ANNA DIXON

ROBERT EADIE

KEITH HENDERSON

STEWART ORR

D. M. RAMSAY

W. SOMERVILLE SHANKS

JOHN G. SPENCE SMITH

A. GORDON THOMAS

A. P. THOMSON

JAMES WRIGHT

MARGARET WRIGHT

BOTHWELL CASTLE

A. P. Thomson

This ruin of a fourteenth-century construction still bears testimony to the men who built it, with its fifteen-foot-thick walls, its towers, its ruined chapel, its ditch, and its dungeon. It was a Murray domain in its early days, and it has the unhappy memory of having acted as headquarters for an English Governor of Scotland. It has been in its time the property of Douglases, of Ramsays, of Hepburns, and of Homes. But the picture that the ruins have for me is of three gentle English people visiting the place on a pleasant August day in the year 1803. William Wordsworth himself unyokes the horse at the stables of the modern Bothwell Castle, and then he, his sister Dorothy, and Coleridge gaze on what the lady describes as 'the ruined castle embosomed in trees'. So Dorothy continues:

'The Castle stands nobly, overlooking the Clyde. When we came up to it I was hurt to see that flower-borders had taken the place of the natural overgrowings of the ruin, the scattered stones and wild plants. It is a large and grand pile, of red freestone, harmonizing perfectly with the rocks of the river, from which, no doubt, it has been hewn. When I was a little accustomed to the unnaturalness of a modern garden, I could not help admiring the excessive beauty and luxuriance of some of the plants. If Bothwell Castle had not been close to the Douglas mansion we should have been disgusted with the possessor's miserable conception of "adorning" such a venerable ruin; but it is so very near to the house that of necessity the pleasure-grounds must have extended beyond it, and perhaps the neatness of a shaven lawn and the complete desolation natural to a ruin might have made an unpleasing contrast; and besides, being within the precincts of the pleasure-grounds, and so very near to the modern mansion of a noble family, it has forfeited in some degree its independent majesty, and becomes a tributary to the mansion; its solitude being interrupted, it has no longer the same command over the mind in sending it back into past times, or excluding the ordinary feelings which we bear about us in daily life. We had then only to regret that the castle and house were so near to each other; and it was impossible not to regret it; for the ruin presides in state over the river, far from city or town, as if it might have had a peculiar privilege to preserve its memorials of past ages and maintain its own character and independence for centuries to come.'

GOUROCK FROM TOWER HILL

Margaret Wright

The point from which the artist has painted this picture is one which provides some of the most pleasant vistas of the Clyde. Roseneath and Helensburgh, Kilmun, the Holy Loch and Dunoon lie stretched out before the spectator, beyond the everlasting movement of the water, and the passing of the ships. And with the eye of memory one can look back four hundred and fifty years, and see down at the old jetty 'Nicholas of Bour, Maister, under God, of the schip called the Verdour', by orders from that great admiral, Andrew Wood of Largo, coming to 'the Goraik, on the west harbour and sey, aucht myles fra Dunbertain', training three hundred men and equipping his ship for war, so as to carry the King probably to the far isles to teach his unruly subjects of the West a lesson.

Then the eye is held by that six-foot-high monolith of grey mica schist standing on the cliff, and known as 'Granny Kempoch'. Its origin is lost in the mist of time, but it was held in superstitious awe by sailors and fishermen of the day before yesterday. Before they set sail, seafarers would pace seven times round it, each man bearing a basket full of sea-sand, and singing a song. So did he hope to protect himself from the anger of the winds and waves. But the devil, that was in men's minds, took a hand in the game, and in 1662 a poor unfortunate lassie of eighteen years of age, Mary Lamont by name, was one of a group of women, who were forced to tell that by this stone they met the devil, danced with him, and were kissed by him; and that their intention had been to cast the stone into the sea so that ships might be destroyed. So Mary and her friends were burned as witches.

But there was a pleasant happening some thirty years later when a Glasgow merchant, Walter Gibson by name, set up a business where red herrings were first prepared in these islands. That was a good first-foot.

HILLHEAD BOWLING GREEN

D. M. Ramsay

A bowling-green in Hillhead! J. J. Bell was born in Hillhead, and he once wrote for me that when he was a boy in that 'suburb, then a burgh, with its own administration, police, fire-brigade, and so on . . . there was still, here and there, extensive plots, which served very well as playgrounds for the numerous children.' That was the time when a Scottish G. K. Chesterton might have written a Scottish 'Napoleon of Notting Hill', or rather 'Hillhead'. And J. J. B. went on to tell how Hillhead was 'though not unhomely, a superior sort of place, the inhabitants generally being both bein and douce—two words with delicacies of meaning not to be gained from the dictionary. It would seem that they were not without a certain naïve snobbery. Many of them did not wish to be identified with a common Street, and nearly every street was divided up into Terraces, Places, Buildings—you may yet discern the faded gold lettering on certain corners—and nearly everybody declared his or her address accordingly, to the confounding of stranger visitors, and the miserable confusion of little boy and girl messengers, new to the district, especially on dark evenings'. Bell tells how his father—the family address was 3 Great Kelvin Terrace—one night met 'a weary weeping little boy, with a laden basket, seeking vainly for some bumptious Buildings or pompous Place. Thenceforth plain "8 Bank Street" was added to the notepaper, and all tradesmen instructed accordingly.'

A green and pleasant place the Hillhead Bowling Green. A green and pleasant memory J. J. Bell. He was warm-hearted, he was kindly, he believed in natural goodness: in his belief in that natural goodness, he gave freely of all he had to all men. He wrote for a living, and much that he wrote he was not really interested in seeing again. But to everything he wrote, he gave care and thought, as he gave care and thought to everybody for whom or to whom he wrote. I always think that was the reason for the courtesy of his beautiful handwriting.

While J. J. Bell was a man of many friends, yet there was something lonely about him. He seems somehow in place alone on Gasgeir Mor, or behind that high garden wall in the Great Glen. Even when I walked with him in St. Andrews, I felt that he might have been a kindly monk, who was to pass from me to something less worldly behind the grey walls—although he would not go without leaving his blessing. And it was thus he passed out of this life, leaving that kindly, twisted smile, that may remind us of the duties we have of kindness to others.

AUCHANDALL—INVERNESS-SHIRE

Keith Henderson

The Field of the Blind Man—who that blind man was, we do not know; when he lived, we do not know. But he is immortalized in a hill, a stream, and a farm that have their place on that stretch of moorland which lies between High Bridge and Fort William. The farm, which bears his name, was there on that pleasant afternoon of the sixteenth day of August 1745; and, if the blind man had been in the vicinity at that time, his ears would have registered a skirl of the pipes, probably the most romantic skirl a piper ever blew into Scots history.

The farm in our picture lies beside the road which Wade made from Fort George in Inverness to Fort William, and a gay company passed by it one Friday in the June of the year 1736. The Governor of the Fort was there with his officers and the local gentry. They were on their way to see the laying of the foundation stone of the High Bridge over the Spean—the bridge which was to complete Wade's work in Scotland. When they reached the site of the bridge, 'the first stone was laid, and the healths of Their Majesties, the Prince and Princess of Wales, The Duke and Royal Family, with many other loyal Toasts were drunk, at the instant our great guns were firing on the happy occasion of the day. . . . The company returned and supped with the Governor, where the above healths were repeated, and the night ended with bonfires, illuminations, and all other demonstrations of joy.'

A noisy business, but not the great noise! That sounded nine years later, up among the trees that hide High Bridge from the Field of the Blind Man. Prince Charlie had landed, and Cope sent off two companies of Sinclair's Royal Scots from Perth to strengthen the garrison in Fort William. Captain John Scot of Scotstarvit in Fife was in command, and set out from Fort Augustus on the morning of 16th August 1745. As his men neared the High Bridge, they heard the sound of the pipes, and saw the colours of the tartan mingling with the green of the leaves. Claymores were waved, war-cries were shouted. Captain Scot withdrew his two fully equipped companies. And yet the enemy all told were but twelve of Keppoch's men, commanded by Donald Macdonald of Tirnadris. The battle of the '45 was joined. The Field of the Blind Man was to suffer much of the marching and counter-marching of war. Now it is lapped in peace.

CASTLE STALKER, APPIN

Stewart Orr

Black against the sunset stands this keep, like a mighty cormorant on the rocks in an arm of the Linnhe Loch in Appin. That it was a hunting-lodge used by James IV a tablet inside the doorway tells, and to that statement the Royal Arms on the wall, though sadly battered by rain and wind and salt air, bear testimony. Duncan Stewart of Appin looked after the keep for his King five hundred years ago. Some writers argue that this name is the straightforward Stalker's Castle, in the sense of the King's deer-stalker dwelling here. Sometimes the name is translated as 'The Castle of the Falconer', but there seems no particular reason why it should not be the Castle of the Dresser of Fish Hooks, which is what the Gaelic word 'Stalcair' means. So we may picture James IV coming to this Appin loch for the peaceful recreation of fishing, sometimes with nets, as his successor George V used to come to Loch Muick and help to drag the trout-heavy net to shore.

But this Castle Stalker has anything but a peaceful story. Stewart and Campbell fought and murdered for it across the centuries. A Stewart (Alexander the Peaceful) holds it till a Campbell (Green Colin) murders him. Then Alexander's son (Donald the Hammerer) kills Green Colin, and so the story goes on.

It is, therefore, with not too happy thoughts that you ascend the outside stair to the first floor of the ruin, and think of those who have lain in the dungeons that comprise the ground floor. The doorway on the first floor gives directly on the great hall, lit from windows on three sides, and with a fireplace on the fourth. A wheeled stair gives access to the two higher storeys.

Many descriptions could be applied to this lonely stone cormorant, but the one used in MacFarlane's *Geographical Collections* comes as something of a surprise: 'A pretty tour in the Appin'.

INTERIOR OF ST. ANDREW'S PARISH CHURCH, GLASGOW

W. Somerville Shanks

In the year 1739 when Wade was first forming the Highland Companies into a regiment of the line, which was to become famous on many fields as the Black Watch, Allan Dreghorn, a Glasgow architect, had completed his plans for the construction of this church, and work had begun on it under that master of master-masons, Mungo Naysmith. Mr. Shanks's picture shows the great beauty of the Corinthian pillars, and the mahogany fronts of the galleries. The visitor will also be impressed by the plaster ornamentation.

The Presbyterian congregation of this church came from a meeting-house named 'The Wynd', which had been opened in 1687. In 1802 William Ritchie was the minister of the charge. He was a man of progressive ideas, and introduced an organ. This action brought down upon his head the anger of the Lord Provost of Glasgow. He took the case before the Presbytery, who expressed the opinion that 'the use of organs in the public worship of God is contrary to the law of the land, and to the law and constitution of our Established Church, and therefore they prohibit it in all chapels and churches within their bounds'. The *Fasti* records that when, in the following year, Doctor Ritchie was translated to Edinburgh High Church, 'a laughable caricature was published, of the venerable minister as an organist playing "I'll gang nae mair to yon Toun".'

ORONSAY PRIORY

W. Marshall Brown

A psychologist would have something to write in this place of the purpose of life, and of the danger of looking back if that purpose is to be fulfilled. The highest point of this Isle Oronsay is called Cairn-cul-n-Ern, the Cairn of the Back Turned to Ireland. Here Columba landed, thinking he had reached his desired haven, but from this hill he could still see Ireland, and so he set out once more in his frail coracle.

Pennant visited this isle in 1772, and wrote of it as follows:

'The ship arrives soon after, and anchors within Gbudimal, which, with two or three other little rocky isles, forms an harbour. After about a mile's walk reach the ruins of the ancient monastery, founded (as some say) by St. Columba, but with more probability by one of the Lords of the Isles, who fixed here a priory of Canons regular of Augustine, dependent on the Abbey of Holyrood, in Edinburgh. The church is fifty-nine feet by eighteen, and contains the tombs of numbers of the ancient islanders, two of warriors recumbent, seven feet long. . . .

'In a side-chapel, beneath an arch, lies an abbot, of the name of Mac-dufie, with two of his fingers elated, in the attitude of benediction; in the same place is a stone enriched with foliage, a stag surrounded with dogs, and a ship with full sail: round is inscribed

HIC JACET MURCHARDUS MAC-DUFIE DE COLLANSA,
AN. DO. 1539, MENSE MART. ORA ME ILLE.   AMMEN.

'This Murchardus is said to have been a great oppressor, and that he was executed, by order of the Lord of the Isles, for his tyranny. Near his tomb is a long pole, placed there in memory of the ensign-staff of the family, which had been preserved miraculously for two hundred years: on it (report says) depended the fate of the Macdufient race, and probably the original perished with this Murchardus.

'Adjoining to the church is the cloister: a square of forty-one feet; one of the sides of the inner wall is ruined; on two of the others are seven low arches, one seven feet high, including the columns, which are nothing more than two thin stones, three feet high, with a flat stone on the top of each, serving as a plinth; and on them two other thin stones, meeting at top, and forming an acute angle, by way of arch: on the fore-side are five small round arches; these surround a court of twenty-eight feet eight inches: the whole of the cloister part had been once covered. This form is peculiar (in our part of Europe) to this place; but I am told that the same form is observed in some of those in the islands of the Archipelago.

'Several other buildings join this, all in a ruinous state; but a most elegant cross is yet standing, twelve feet high, one foot seven broad, five inches thick.'

Ormskirk Priory. 1910.

Marshall Browne.

IONA CATHEDRAL

Stewart Orr

There are two people in whose company I should like to visit Iona—Neil Gunn and Samuel Johnson. Each has a particular understanding of the place, Neil Gunn because of all the race that lives through him into understanding, and Samuel Johnson because of all the humanity that lives through him into understanding. I would go with Gunn by 'the way the brethren walked to their work, over the back of the island, to the Machair in front of the great western bay', near which they met 'the incomparable gladness'. We would come back to the knoll where Columba communed with the angels, and there Gunn would reconstruct for me Columba's 'outside face with its leadership upon it. Irony to serenity to the true humility, in which the flesh over the bone and the irises of the eyes are purified of the insignia of the boss—it is difficult to get the face of a leader like that, apart, perhaps from the faces of one or two great religious leaders out of the East. And nothing less quite satisfies a mood grown weary of all the personal humours or manifestations of egoism. As though a modern voice cried with the agony of a pure spirit: " Hell, let us be shut of all that egoism meantime".' I should like to go with Gunn to the place where Columba discovered he could no longer see Ireland; I should ask Gunn to talk of the Druids and of Oran's burial. I should gaze with him at the great Cross, and feel 'the harmony behind the chisel that hewed it'. And with him I think I should understand how the best of the Druid and the best of the Cross might meet on a stone.

But now to land with Dr. Johnson in the late evening from Maclean's strong boat on the shoulders of strong clansmen. 'Whatever withdraws us', says the Doctor, 'from the power of our sense, whatever makes the past, the distant, or the future predominate over the present, advances us in the dignity of thinking beings. . . . The man is little to be envied whose patriotism would not gain force upon the plain of Marathon or whose piety would not grow warmer among the ruins of Iona'.

We spend the night with the Doctor and Boswell in that barn full of hay, and in the morning we 'rise and survey the place'—the church, the chapel of the nunnery, used as a cow-house, the crosses, and the burial-place of the Kings. 'The graves are very numerous', says Johnson, 'and some of them undoubtedly contain the remains of men who did not expect to be so soon forgotten'.

So the islanders push our boat into the water, and now we leave 'these illustrious ruins, by which Mr. Boswell was much affected, nor would I willingly be thought to have looked upon them without some emotion. Perhaps, in the revolutions of the world, Iona may be some time again the instructress of the Western regions.'

KISHMUL CASTLE, BARRA

Anna Dixon

A book could be written about the island-fortresses of Scotland, which have housed so many pirates, plunderers, and others. You find them in inland lochs, such as the castle on the island in Loch an Eilean, whence the Wolf of Badenoch used to issue on his nefarious raids. The Wolf passed with his kind, and then that other sort of raider, the osprey, built its castle in the ruins. But in turn it became the prey of other robbers—and now all are gone. The most famous castle of this type in a sea-loch is Kishmul in Castlebay, Barra. The Norsemen seem to have had some kind of fortification here, but we have no actual date for the original building, though, if you put the age of the present castle at one thousand years, you would not be far out. It is built of local stone, and has an outer wall enclosing what were once inhabited quarters. The tower is rectangular and is said to have once contained a chapel. Dr Donald Buchanan, writing in 1942, says he was informed by the factor to the Barra estates that ' the ruins of a chapel, with half an altar-stone fractured across its reliquary receptacle, and other harmonising relics of worship, have been discovered in the castle during a survey preliminary to restoration.' There was a well, and Martin, who visited the island in 1695, states: 'There is a little magazine in the tower, to which no stranger has access'.

The Macneils came to Barra somewhere about the beginning of the fifteenth century, and the tenth of the line was Rory the Tartar. He was a pretty complete pirate, meeting full approval of his clan, and we like to remember that, when the Tutor of Kintail captured him by a trick, and took him to Edinburgh in 1604 to answer for his piratical habits, Rory claimed that he had seized one of Queen Elizabeth's ships and carried off the cargo, because of the English Queen's treatment of the Scottish King's mother. He was pardoned. The seventeenth chief, General Roderick Macneil, had his estates sold by his creditors in 1838. He was the last Macneil of Barra, and the chiefship passed to a family of Macneils who lived on Prince Edward Island. By the law of Tanistry the present chief is Robert Lister Macneil of Barra, whose position was established by the Lyon King in 1915, and who repurchased the greater part of Barra along with Kishmul Castle.

It is pleasant to remember of this place that 'Kishmul's Galley' and 'Kishmul's Cradle-Song' are two of the loveliest melodies in Mrs. Marjory Kennedy-Fraser's collections.

TAYNUILT CHURCH

John G. Spence Smith

'A cattle-hold for sunbeams' is a translation of the Gael's description of Glen Etive at the foot of which stands this church of Taynuilt. A church was first built here at Muckairn early in the thirteenth century by Harald, first Bishop of Argyll, and there were two old chapels near here, St. Ronan's at Kilmavonaig and St. Mary's at Kilvorie; but in the imagination the music of the psalm dies away in this place before the singing of Ireland's Helen, that Deirdre of the Sorrows, whom the King of Erin desired to marry, for she was the fairest maid in all the lands of the Gael. Deirdre fled with her lover, Naoise, to Alba and to Glen Etive. But the King of Erin persuaded the lovers to return home, and there they met death, and the bard cried:

Awake, Darthula, awake thou first of women! The wind of spring is abroad. The flowers shake their heads on the green hills. The woods wave their growing leaves. Retire, O sun! The daughter of Colla is asleep. She will not come forth in her beauty. She will not move in the steps of her loveliness.

Just beyond Taynuilt lies Colleanaish, the wood of Naoise, and behind it Glen Lonain, where Deirdre listened to the calling of the cuckoo. The woods around here were burned to make charcoal for smelting purposes. In the old days the Gaelic deer-stalkers had their arrow heads tipped 'at the smiddy of Macfeadern in Earcle by Bonawe', and iron furnaces were working here at the time of Trafalgar. It was workmen from those furnaces who set up in this place the earliest monument in Scotland to Lord Nelson.

But the church is here with the trees around for what this glen stands for—not war but peace.

THE GIANT CRANE

A. Gordon Thomas

Down the slopes of Queensberry Hill in Lanarkshire, laughing and tumbling, comes a trickle of water. In that high land of our Lowlands they have named it the Crook Burn, but further down they call it Daer Water, and near Elvanfoot it meets a similar volume of water christened the Clydes Burn, and the two as one take to themselves the name of Clyde. This Clyde has a happy childhood in pleasant places, where the angler can take his trout, and where in spring 'blown blossom-boats from fruit trees sail on the ripples'. All the wide district pours its waters into it, waters with the lovely names of Elvan, Midlock and Camps, Glengonar, Duneaton, Lamington. As it nears the town of Biggar, another great river a few miles away, the Tweed, has decided to turn to the east. A little further on the Douglas Water throws in its lot, so that it can have the fun of dashing over the rocks that make the Falls of Clyde, that make the Linns of Bonnington, Corra, Dundaff, and Stonebyres. In a gracious tract of land the Clyde accepts the Avon's company, and then it comes to the real region of towns, as it flows under the bridge on the road between Hamilton and Motherwell. It shudders somewhat as Bothwell Bridge is reflected in its waters. So it goes by Blantyre, Uddingston, and Cambuslang, by Rutherglen and Glasgow Green, to the Broomielaw: then by the quays of the great Harbour of Glasgow, and to a point where the somewhat grimy Kelvin joins it, and tells it of memories of Kelvingrove: by the Fairfield yards, and Scotstoun, by Renfrew, and then with the tale of Paisley brought to it by the River Cart, by Clydebank and Dalmuir, by Dumbuck and Dumbarton, where the Leven comes with its word of Ben Lomond, by Cardross and Greenock, by Helensburgh and Gourock, and so away southwards into its mighty Firth.

That giant crane and all the ships—from the *Comet* to the *Queen Elizabeth*—of this greatest shipbuilding river in the world, who has best described the scene? I would make choice of that Greenock lad, John Davidson's 'A Ballad in Blank Verse of the Making of a Poet'.

> '. . . . . this grey town
> That pipes the morning up before the lark
> With shrieking steam, and from a hundred stalks
> Lacquers the sooty sky: where hammers clang
> On iron hulls, and cranes in harbours creak,
> Rattle and swing, whole cargoes on their necks.'

THE KNOWE, KILBARCHAN

James Wright

The danger that this interesting old steeple might be destroyed by a German bomb has passed, but, at the time of writing, there is a threat that subsidence of the ground may necessitate the removal of the building. Some of the old houses in the picture have already gone, and, should the steeple join them, then the statue of Habbie Simpson, which stands in a niche in one of its walls, will also go. Kilbarchan folk are all 'Habbies', but Habbie Simpson was the most kenspeckle of them all. He was a piper, rival of Rab the Ranter, who figures in Tennant's 'Anster Fair', and, as in the case of Rab, a poet has sung of him. That poet was Robert Sempill of Beltrees, eldest son of Sir James Sempill, named after James VI, who, as an infant, became his god-father, and 'at whose feet (no, at whose elbow, and from whose mouth) I confess', wrote Sir James, 'I have sucht the best of whatsoever may be thought good in me'.

Habbie Simpson lived in the early years of the seventeenth century, and, when he wasn't acting as the local butcher, he was playing the pipes, and he did not allow his business as flesher to interfere with his interests in music. He fiddled at all the weddings, at harvest-homes, at the fairs, when stage-plays were held in the open air, at horse-races. James Sempill's grandson wrote of Habbie that

'He had a son and kept a servant. Both of them he taught to play, and came that length, that on a wedding day he played the newest tune, and then laid his pipes by, and ordered his son and servant to play the rest, and himself sat down at the bride's table.'

There was in existence at one time an oil-painting of Habbie, and, using it as an original, Archibald Robertson, a Greenock wood-carver, executed the wooden statue which was placed in the niche of the steeple in 1821. Habbie had one other quality which would have endeared him to many people had he been living to-day. As the poet Sempill writes:

> He counted was a weil'd Wight-man,
> And fiercely at Foot-ba' he ran;
> At ev'ry game the gree he wan,
>   For Pith and Speed,
> The like of Habbie was na than,
>   But now he's dead.

TRACE HORSES

Robert Eadie

The great city of Glasgow has always been so busy on its lawful occasions that it has been somewhat careless of its personal appearance. It has been a kind of vigorously growing plant that has spread over a great area, and has never been pruned. That sprawling growth has been such that you do not realize that Glasgow is a city built upon hills with a silver river in the valley. It has many fine Victorian buildings, but they all suggest utility of purpose. Mr. Eadie's picture of this part of West Nile Street makes an ideal cross-section of a community. There is a suggestion of purpose about everything and everybody—the tram-lines, the motor-car, and the shoppers—and, lastly, the trace-horses waiting and ready for their job of giving the extra power to heavy traffic, the destination of which is away up one of those hills of Glasgow on which Buchanan Street Station finds itself. But, curiously enough, horses labouring in a city are connected in my mind with the Sabbath. Many years ago, when I was a very small boy, my father took me walking in some part of the green belt that surrounded a great Scottish city. We came to a field, and it was full of those city horses taking their Sunday rest. I can still see the sunshine splashing on their backs through the leaves of green trees, and the whisking of their tails. It was that complete enjoyment of peace after work well done. It was a proof of the Divine wisdom that labour could be for six days, but that the seventh day had been put aside for rest, and that the Divine gift of that reserved day was a right for all living things who must toil. There was also the sense of rehabilitation for that toil, and of the renewed vigour which even the city horses would feel when the traces tightened on their huge shoulders on the Monday morning.

Glasgow streets! How they keep their tradition! It is the best part of a century ago since William Black wrote:

'This golden-radiant city of Glasgow! with its thousand activities all awakening to join the noise and din of the joyous morning, and its over-arching skies full of a white light of hope and gladness and fair assurance of the future. The clerks and warehousemen were hurrying by to their desks and counters: work-folk were leisurely getting home for their well-earned breakfast: smart young men and slim-waisted women were already setting the shop windows to rights: great lorries were clattering their loads of long iron bars through the crowded streets; and omnibuses and tramway cars and railway trains were bringing in from all points of the compass their humming freight of eager human bees to this mighty and dusky hive. But dusky it did not appear to him as he was speedily making his way across the town towards his brother's home. It was all transfigured and glorified—the interminable thoroughfares, the sky-piercing chimneys, the masses of warehouses, the overhead network of telegraph lines, the red-funnelled steamers moving slowly away through the pale blue mist of the Broomielaw: all these were spectral in a strange kind of way, yet beautiful: and he could not but think that the great mass of this busy multitude was well content with the pleasant morning, and the nebulous pale-golden sunlight, and the glimpses of long cirrus cloud hanging far above the city's smoke.'

And that is Glasgow to-day!

NORTH AND CENTRAL SCOTLAND

Artists

STEWART CARMICHAEL

ANNA DIXON

ALBERT C. DODDS

ROBERT EADIE

DAVID FOGGIE

W. M. FRAZER

MARTIN HARDIE

VIOLET M. KAY

ALEXANDER MACPHERSON

SIR JOHN STIRLING MAXWELL, BART.

JAMES MILLER

ROBERT B. NISBET

JAMES RITCHIE

ROBERT C. ROBERTSON

JOHN G. SPENCE SMITH

A. P. THOMSON

JAMES WRIGHT

MARGARET WRIGHT

AULD BRIG OF EARN

W. M. Frazer

In the dreich days of October and November 1856, an artist put up his easel under the new Bridge of Earn, and proceeded to paint in the Auld Brig as a background for a picture which was to cause much controversy in its day. The artist took some liberties with that background, for he introduced Elcho Castle—a building some distance away on the bank of the Tay—for the sake of his composition. The artist was John Everett Millais, and the picture was his 'Sir Isumbras at the Ford', in which he depicts that knight, shorn of his pride by the attacks of savage circumstance, in his humility bearing on his war-horse the two children of a wood-cutter across the waters. Certain critics frowned on the picture, and Fred Sands drew a parody of it in which the war-horse has become an ass, branded J. R. Oxon (John Ruskin); Millais himself is given the place of Sir Isumbras, while the wood-cutter's children are represented by D. G. Rossetti and Holman Hunt.

Millais introduced nuns into the background of his picture, and those ladies recall to us the original builders of the Auld Brig of Earn. They were monks from Balmerino Abbey, who, in the twelfth century, constructed this bridge so that they might have easy access to Perth and Perthshire where they owned considerable properties. Their bridge is probably the oldest arched bridge in Scotland, but only two of the original five arches are extant.

The Auld Brig of Earn has had many people who considered it their care. Robert Bruce made the Abbot of Scone responsible for keeping the structure in repair, while James VI gave the city fathers of Perth the right to levy tolls, by the expending of which the bridge might be kept in good condition. But at length the old bridge became so tired of feet crossing and recrossing it, that it refused to be patched up any longer. It was 'through the piece', as we say in Scotland. So they left it alone to dream of other days, and they built the new bridge in 1822.

BRIDGE OF FASNAKYLE, INVERNESS-SHIRE

Albert C. Dodds

This Fasnakyle Bridge in this book stands as representative of all the bridges in the Highlands of Scotland, which not only lead to the glories of that fine land, but which, in themselves, are stopping-places, points of view. Fasnakyle stands near the point where the Affaric becomes the Glass, midway between that wild and beautiful track west to Kintail, and that kindly road east to Beauly. Standing on this bridge the mind can so easily travel back those two hundred odd years to an early August morning, when a party of weary fugitives, Prince Charlie in their midst, took refuge here 'in a very fast wood', where they remained hidden for three days. And the person we like to remember as we stand on the bridge is John Chissolm, the farmer at Fasnakyle, who kept the Prince and his party going in 'meal, butter, and cheese, and flesh . . . Aquavitae and tabaco'. Here is how the story is told in *The Lyon in Morning*:

'When at Fassanacoill, the farmer there, John Chissolm, used to furnish Patrick Grant, and the other provisors with meat and drink for themselves and their company; John Chissolm, in the meantime, knowing nothing at all about the Prince. When the Prince heard that John Chissolm had furnished him with provisions, he desired that John might be brought to him; and accordingly Patrick Grant and Hugh Macmillan were dispatched to John Chissolm with that intent. They desired John to come along with them to see a friend whom he would like very well to see without telling who the friend was. John answered, "I believe there is some person of consequence amongst you, and as I have one bottle of wine (the property of a priest with whom I am in very great friendship), I will venture to take it along with me." Patrick Grant said, "What! John, Have you had a bottle of wine all this time and not given it to us before this time?" Away they went to the Prince, whom John Chisholm knew at first sight, having been in his army. Upon delivering the bottle of wine to the Prince, Patrick Grant desired the favour of his Royal Highness to drink to him (Patrick Grant) for, added he, "I do not remember that your Royal Highness has drunken to me since you came among our hands." Accordingly the Prince put the bottle of wine to his mouth and drank a health to Patrick Grant and all friends. John Chissolm having received good payment for any provisions he had furnished, and finding they had been purchased for the use of his Prince, immediately offered to return the whole price, and pressed the thing much. But the Prince would not hear of that at all, and ordered him to keep the money.'

DUNDEE FROM THE OLD STEEPLE

Stewart Carmichael

I cannot recall the name of any other city or town in these islands which has a descriptive adjective attached to it in the same way as Dundee has attached to it the adjective 'bonnie'. The evidence is absolutely conclusive that the adjective was applied to the town long before John Graham became Viscount Dundee. Old pictures, like those by Sleezer, show us in truth a Dundee that was fair to look upon, when, as we read in that old anonymous poem 'Tayis Bank', down somewhere by Dock Street

> The nightingale woik off her nest
> Singing, the day updawis.

But that was before lums and railways had seamed and wrinkled the bonnie face.

Yet, I now ask you to climb with me on a November evening from the centre of this one-time bonnie city on a road which leads to the west, a road closed at its far end by a barrier of fire that blazes from the furnace of the departing sun. We move behind a façade of middle-class respectability through a wilderness of slums where mills, loan-offices and second-hand shops all jostle each other as they crowd in to watch the happenings on the road. As we reach the heights, the spires of the city churches are a translucent opal where they taper into the green sky, and suddenly we realize that the mill and factory buildings, which push on to the pavements, are emptied of all menace and noise.

Or, shall we take a road to the north on an April morning, when, as we climb higher and higher, we look back every now and again to a sudden glint of glistening river, and a splash of green on the waterside braes of Fife: or, if in the evening we should cross to those braes and look back on Dundee, we shall see a fairyland of fireflies, and great swords of yellow light driven deep into the blue-black waters of the Tay?

Come with me now right to the top of the high-ground of Dundee, to the summit of the Law, where yesterday and to-day join hands in the War Memorial built on a Pictish dun. Here we can survey the whole city. To the south of us the old town smokes from the old chimneys above the houses crowding together like old, old friends, and gazing out on the river, remembering Alectum; to the north the new chimneys stand singly here and there in pleasant meadow-land, with the clusters of new little towns, the suburbs of the working-folk, stretching back to the hills of the fairies—the Sidlaws. To the east the docks and shipbuilding yards fringe on the mansions of Broughty Ferry, and beyond stretch out those links with as good golf courses as are to be found anywhere; while, to the west, lie the orchards and fields of the pleasant Carse of Gowrie. A 'bonnie' town indeed!

DUNNET KIRK, CAITHNESS

David Foggie

Situated in that area of Caithness which is the most northerly part of the British mainland, Dunnet Kirk is a unique example of a Scottish mediaeval Parish Church. Much of the original features remain, although the mediaeval doorway has been built up, the old-time galleries have disappeared, and a new aisle was added about 1830. In the tower you will still find the original circular stairway, and on another stairway a memorial to the most famous of all the ministers of the parish—Timothy Pont. That extraordinary man is credited with Venetian forebears, and his father was Robert Pont of Culross, who was educated at the University of St. Andrews, and became Minister of Dunkeld. Later he became a Senator of the College of Justice, and Minister of St. Cuthbert's, Edinburgh. His son, Timothy, was entered as a student at St. Leonard's College, St. Andrews, in 1579, and graduated there in 1583. He was Minister of Dunnet from 1601 to 1608, and in that last year he set out on his feet to explore the whole of Scotland, he being 'a complete mathematician'. He made, on the spot, surveys of all the Scottish counties, and islands. With his work almost completed, he died somewhere about 1630, but his records were 'in great danger from moths and vermin through the carelessness of his relatives'. Sir John Scot of Scotstarvit, took the matter in hand, had Robert Gordon of Straloch and his son, James Gordon of Rothiemay, revise Pont's originals, and they were published in Bleau's Atlas at Amsterdam in 1662. The originals of Pont's surveys are preserved in the National Library of Scotland.

ELGIN CATHEDRAL

Sir John Stirling Maxwell, Bart.

This 'Lantern of the North' is remembered not so much now for the light that was shed from it, as for the numerous occasions on which the glass has been broken and that light extinguished. The sacred 'Lamp' was first lit on a beautiful summer's day in July 1224, with High Mass, and a Papal Bull, the Bishop of Caithness consecrating and Bishop Andrew Moray left in charge. Five lofty towers rose to the sky, but in fifty years fire left them standing 'naked to their enemies'. Now that all is understood, he no doubt sleeps sound enough under his massive stone in Dunkeld Cathedral, but the Wolf of Badenoch swept in his living restlessness down on this cathedral in 1390, and, some say, levelled even the towers. Twelve years later the son of the Lord of the Isles plundered the place, and in the following centuries Dunbars and Inneses—a plague on both their houses—desecrated the place with their feuds. Regent Moray tore the lead from the roof, and in 1637 'ane horrible high wind' blew down the rafters. Cromwell's troopers may have taken a hand in the ultimate destruction, and on Easter Sunday, 1711, the great tower fell.

So let us to something kindlier. Let us pass amid to-day's ruins beneath the arch of the aisle of St. Columba into what is left of the Chapter House, and across it to the Lavatory, a small chamber in which we shall find the basin-trough that contained water in which the officiating priest washed his hands before celebrating Mass. In 1748 that trough became a baby's cradle. There was a lass, Marjory Gilzean, who loved and was loved by a soldier named Anderson, quartered in Elgin in 1745. The old story of angry parents, and the lass away with the lad, and back again in three years with a bairn, a broken heart, and a deranged mind! There is no place for her to lay her head, so she seeks the priests' Lavatory, the baby is laid in the trough, and there she dwells till the baby is old enough to go to school as a 'pauper'. He cleans the schoolroom, as payment for his teaching. Then he is apprenticed to an uncle, runs away, joins the East India Company as a drummer, and leaves these shores. The mother, too, went wandering, but only up and down the Moray country-side, and in 1790 she died and was buried. Twenty-one years later the boy returns to Elgin—a Major-General. In time he, too, dies, but he leaves his fortune of £70,000 to build and endow the 'Elgin Institution for the Support of Old Age and Education of Youth'. Another 'Lantern of the North' is lit, the light of which has not been put out.

112

DUNKELD CATHEDRAL

Robert C. Robertson

Buttressed tower, traceried spiracles, Gothic arches with fluted soffits, Norman pillars, crocketed pinnacles, all crowd together in this half-ruin by the banks of Tay. Half-ruin, for the choir of this cathedral still serves as a church—with a strange ancestry. Here in the sixth century, the Culdees constructed their wattle building; some hundred years later stone took the place of the intertwined branches, and in 848 Kenneth Macalpine built a new church, to serve as a sepulchre for Columba, whose bones, it is said, the King had brought from Iona. The 'sair sanct' was the monarch who combined monastery and kirk in a bishopric, and in the following three hundred and fifty years bishop after bishop added to the building. But the completed house had scarcely a hundred years of life when the winds of the Reformation blew upon it, and it fell. In 1820, however, the then Duke of Atholl converted the choir into a usable kirk.

If Columba, the dove, sleeps here, he has some strange bed-fellows. A mighty effigy in armour tells us here the restless Wolf of Badenoch rests; a bishop dreams under a croketed canopy; a statue keeps in our memory that other bishop 'Carney', who thrashed the English thrice in one day; there is a tablet to tell of that gallant minister, John Robb, who played so heroic a part on board the *Forfarshire*, but died before Grace Darling's boat came to the rescue; that plain stone there informs that underneath lies Count Roehenstart (General Charles Edward Stuart), a grandson of Bonnie Prince Charlie, and son of the Duchess of Albany; that other plain stone is a memorial to William Cleland, the great Covenanter, and first Colonel of the Cameronians (Scottish Rifles), who waited here for Claverhouse's army, fresh from its victory at Killiecrankie. Cleland had been marching north to join Mackay, but was too late for the battle in the Pass. So he put Dunkeld—village, cathedral and mansion-house—in a state of defence, and, though vastly outnumbered, the Cameronians fought on. Cleland was killed, but the Highland army slowly disintegrated, and vanished into the recesses of the northern mountains. So Claverhouse and Cleland, students of the same College at the beginning of life in St. Andrews, died similar deaths close to each other in the hour of their victories, and both sleep by kirks in Atholl.

Durham Cathedral
Robert C. Martin

GATEWAY TO KENMORE

Margaret Wright

> Admiring Nature in her wildest grace,
> These northern scenes with weary feet I trace;
> O'er many a winding dale and painful steep,
> Th' abodes of covey'd grouse and timid sheep,
> My savage journey, curious, I pursue,
> Till fam'd Breadalbane opens to my view.

So wrote Burns 'with my pencil over the chimney-piece in the parlour of the inn at Kenmore, at the outlet of Loch Tay'. We have a long record of an inn in that model village nestling (or crouching) in the shadow of Taymouth Castle. Let me introduce you to Hew Hay and his wife, Christian Stannes, who, some four hundred years ago, acquired the lease of an inn in Kenmore from Grey Colin (the grandson of the first Campbell laird of Breadalbane) which he had built on the Ferry Croft. The inn had a loft, chimneys, doors, and windows; and Grey Colin was determined it should be well run, for Hew and Christian were to forfeit the lease if bread and ale—and those in generous quantities—were not always awaiting the weary traveller. And when the traveller asked for his bill, there was to be no overcharging.

It was Grey Colin who built the first Campbell home here in a grove of blackthorn and hawthorn where the first thrush was heard. It was at the furthest east point of the property, and it was Colin's idea to 'birse yont'. But, although fifty years ago Mr. J. L. Robertson wrote in *Punch* from Ben Lawers:

> From Kenmore
> to Ben More
> The land is a' the Markiss's,

yet the Breadalbane Campbells 'birsed yont' never a step. The gate in the picture, which leads from the village to the castle, has seen many of the great pass beneath its arch. Now they come through it to play golf, or in the castle halls where Victoria and Albert danced, and where the bombs of taxation ended 'an auld sang', to learn how to avoid destruction from the bombs of the war of to-morrow.

HALF-TIDE, ROSSIE ISLAND, MONTROSE

Robert B. Nisbet

In several of the old country houses of Angus you will find preserved paper-knives and other such articles made from the wood of an old ship, which, running aground on its shores, brought Rossie Island into history. That island divides the river South Esk into two channels where it enters the North Sea south of Montrose. In the year 1745 Montrose, although small—it contained some four thousand inhabitants—was a pleasant, thriving, and not unimportant seaport. It was from that port in 1715 that Old Mr. Melancholy had said good-bye for ever to Scotland after Sheriffmuir, and boarded the *Maria Theresa* of St. Maloes, and in 1745 the Government sent John Byng, Rear-Admiral of the Blue, to watch Montrose and other east-coast ports in case the Old Pretender's son received help from ships using them from the Continent, or, should he be defeated, escaped like his father from one of them. It had been rumoured that a French privateer lay in Montrose Basin, and Byng despatched H.M.S. *Hazard* (Captain Thomas Hill) to destroy the Frenchman, and to immobilize all merchantmen lying in Montrose basin. Hill found no French sloop, and proceeded to dismantle the local vessels. But the Jacobites were in power in Montrose, and one night they crossed from the Town to Rossie Island—at low water the channel almost dries up. The following afternoon, under cover of fog, a French frigate sailed into the Basin and landed some French officers, 150 men of Lord John Drummond's regiment, and six heavy brass cannon. The vessel was then run aground on Rossie Island, where the Jacobites raised a battery, and proceeded to bombard the *Hazard*. It was a Sunday, and the folk at service in Maryton Kirk grew so excited that they rushed out and left the minister to preach to empty pews. Next day Hill surrendered the *Hazard* to the Jacobites. The same night another French frigate, *Le Fine*, arrived and landed Lord John Drummond and 300 officers and men. The *Hazard* was re-named the *Prince Charles*: the French captain, who had run his ship on Rossie Island, was given command, and he sailed from Montrose in the end of January and made Dunkirk. The remains of the French frigate lay for thirty years on Rossie Island, when what was left of her had to be removed because of silting. And she became paper-knives and other articles. So ended one of the few naval incidents of the Jacobite Risings.

KILDRUMMIE CASTLE

Martin Hardie

Thirty-five miles from Aberdeen on the Donside Road stands the Castle of Kildrummie. Part of it has been standing there for nigh eight hundred years, for the date of the construction of the oldest part of it is given as 1172. It was the strong-point of the Garioch, that 150 square miles of territory known as 'the granary of Aberdeenshire'. The Garioch was the property of David, Earl of Huntingdon, brother of William the Lion, and the castle is said to have been a kind of defensive work against the raids of the Norsemen. Somewhere about 1230, Gilbert, who was Bishop of Caithness and Treasurer to Alexander II, built seven additional towers on the castle. Freestone was the material used on the double walls, the outer of which was some nine and the inner some four foot wide, and the general layout was a five-storey-high central tower, known as the Snow Tower, with other small towers and buildings in between, all circling an inner courtyard. One of those buildings was a chapel. There was also a great hall, the foundations of which, as well as those of the chapel, can still be traced. Cordiner, writing in 1776, records that there was a massive chain suspended from the top of the great tower, 'and reaching to the ground for the more commodiously raising water for the use of the upper apartments. Some old men, who remember when the chain was taken away, say there was a deep well underneath.' Wallace was here, and here Bruce found a refuge for his Queen after Methven. But Edward I sent forces to besiege the castle, and they burned out the defenders. It was, however, rebuilt, and withstood another siege by the Earl of Atholl in 1335. The Wolf of Badenoch came ravishing this way, and married the widow of the owner, Sir Malcolm Drummond, who had been murdered some time previously. The castle became a ruin during the Cromwellian wars, and took its place, in the natural Scottish course of events, as the local quarry. Many of the buildings in the district contain stones raped from Kildrummie. Mr. Hardie's picture shows the three lancet windows of the chapel, the only part of the building remaining, with claims to some artistic beauty.

A HIGHLAND SMITHY

A. P. Thomson

THE STRONG MAN

There was a King in Micras
  Who ruled a tinker-clan,
And everything about him
  Was the measure of a man.
The strength of both his arm and mind
  Kept all the laws he made.
He took tent of no other laws
  To keep his mind afraid.

I knew a King in Micras,
  Mighty of leg and arm;
So gentle was his spirit,
  It kept him from all harm.
He was a tree wide-spreading
  Beneath whose kindly shade
Was room for all the subject-friends
  That King in Micras made.

I'll go no more to Micras
  Where the tinker-larachs lie;
There hearth-stones cold and open
  To the weeping of the sky.
No trees stand fornent Micras now,
  Nor the King who was a tree;
For Death has locked the Micras door
  And thrown away the key.

KING'S COLLEGE, ABERDEEN

James Ritchie

Here, where I sit, I can hear the hammer strike the hours on the Elizabeth Bell which hangs beside the Katharine Bell in the tower of Bishop Kennedy's Collegiate Church of St. Salvator, and on Sundays those bells ring our remembrance of the Day, and of that Scotsman who was so closely connected in greatness, in ideals, and in patriotism with Bishop Elphinstone, whose Collegiate Church in Aberdeen is surmounted by the crown, which dominates Sir James Ritchie's picture.

The Records of the University of Aberdeen tell us how:

'Bishop William Elphinstone founded the universitie of Aberdene, with the varietie of professours, maisters and members thereof; caused build the magnifick edifice of the colledge, church, professours' houses, and gairdens therein; mortified unto the same the rents and revenues whereon they might then competentlie live for the time; richlie also adorned and endowed the said colledge with costlie ornaments, bells, jewells, tapestrie, and the lyk; and founded twelf bursars of philosophie to be educat in their course of philosophie and pass the degree of maister of airts therein.'

Boece, to whom the building was more familiar than to any other, wrote of that church:

'In the college there is a church, floored with polished and squared stones, with windows, fine carved work, seats for the use of the priests, and benches for the boys, made with wonderful art, marble altars, images of the saints, statues and pictures gilt with gold; chairs of brass; hangings and carpets to cover the walls and floor, that the whole might appear more splendid. It was also magnificently decorated with much other precious furniture.

'There were also a crucifix, two candlesticks, the same number of censers, an incense-boat, six altar cruets, eight chalices, a textuary, two monstrances for holding the Host, in which the Body of Christ is carried to be worshipped by the people; another of the same, two cubits high, of incredibly fine workmanship. Besides these were a finger basin, a receptacle for water, a vessel for carrying the holy water, along with a sprinkler. All these were of gold and silver. There were also several cambric cloths, embroidered with gold and various figures, and others of the finest white linen, interwoven with flowers of various colours. With these the altars are covered in time of service. There, too, is a casket of cypress-wood, set with pearls and jewels, and of beautiful workmanship. In it are kept for veneration the holy relics of the saints set in gold and silver.

'The church has a bell-tower of immense height, with a stone arch in the shape of an imperial crown, built with wonderful art, and raised above the leaden roof. It contains thirteen bells, pleasing the ear with sweet and holy melody. All these were the gift of Bishop William.'

Pleasing to the spirit also is the memory of that man, whose tower, imperially crowned, soars into our northern sky.

MAR'S WARK, STIRLING

Robert Eadie

It is a somewhat tragic business that the remains of this fine town mansion of another day should have become known in many quarters as 'Mar's Wark'.   The word 'Wark' really means 'workhouse', and was first applied to the building by the Town Council of Stirling somewhere about the year 1733, when it was used by that Council as a kind of penal establishment where vagrants and wastrels were forced to work.   During the '45, however, it was practically destroyed, and the Town Council ceased to interest themselves in it.   Later much of it was taken down.

The proper name for the building is 'The Earl of Mar's Lodging'.   It was built originally by the Regent Mar between the years 1567 and 1572, and, after the Regent's death, his widow, and later his son, the Lord High Treasurer, occupied it.   But, once the Stuarts had gone, the Mar family had a thin time of it, and their fortunes, so far as Stirling is concerned, reached the nadir after the '15.

The only remains of this once magnificent edifice are a portion of the front wall, and the underground vaults.   At one time the towers on each side of the main gateway had inside stairs, but it would appear that the main entrance to the Lodging must have been from inside the courtyard.   The panels above the entrance to the towers and above the court arch carry mottoes, one of which reads:

THE · MOIR · I · STAND · ON · OPPIN · HITHT
MY · FAULTIS · MORE · SUBJECT · ARE · TO · SITHT.

MILL, STRATHDON

Anna Dixon

A mill on an Aberdeenshire river brings to my mind the story of a man born in such a mill as is shown in this picture. That man's name was Alexander Davidson, and he first saw the light in the mill of Inver on Deeside in the year 1792. When he grew to man's estate his first employment was as a keeper in the forest of Fealar; then he took to whisky-smuggling, and later to logging on Deeside. He cut his trees in Glen Derry in the Cairngorms, and floated them down the Dee; but the landlord, the Earl of Fife, went bankrupt, and Sandy had to do the same. So he became a kind of 'professional poacher'. Out came his rod in March, and he went for the spring fish where he chose. In the autumn he used a leister, the old salmon-spear. In August he took to the gun, and shot where he pleased.

He always asked leave of the owner of the moor over which he intended to shoot, stating in his request that he would take a straight line across the property, and that he would 'not poach but only kill what may be in my way on my annual tour'. If permission were not granted, well, he shot just the same. The majority of landlords, however, granted Davidson permission to go through their property, for they knew he would keep to his bargain of the straight line. Davidson was also the first Highland dancer of his day, and was welcome in many great houses, where he would partner duchess and dairymaid. When he was found lying dead on the hills of Glenbucket there was found in his pocket an invitation from the Earl of March asking him to attend a ball in Gordon Castle. In Glenmuick churchyard, near Ballater, you will find an undressed headstone with the letters A. D. carved on it. Underneath it Sandy Davidson was laid to rest on an August day in 1843. Rev. J. G. Michie wrote of Davidson thus:

'Without justifying that life (that of the last poacher of the olden type), it is only simple truth to say that in his own eyes it was no violation of the laws of God; and in the eyes of those best capable of judging, it was more the result of a peculiarly romantic and chivalrous turn of mind than of any low or lawless disposition. Whatever be the opinion entertained by some on this matter, no one who knew him intimately—and he had a wider circle of acquaintances than any native of the north of Scotland of his day—will deny to his memory the testimony that he was imbued with the highest sentiments of honour and religion, while his actions were characterised by the strictest integrity of purpose, and the loftiest generosity.'

OLD ABERDEEN

Violet M. Kay

Old Aberdeen is not of such great antiquity as Aberdeen, but since it has retained the grace of a young day, it has been given its title of age. Old Aberdeen and St. Andrews have a unique quality in common; each centres around a college tower, built by a great Scottish Bishop; each had a chapel beside a leper-house; on the bounds of each stands a cathedral; in each are pleasant old houses with pleasant garden ground; there are many place-names held in common, such as Kinkell and St. Nicholas.

There are so many places to be visited in this old Aberdeen—that little graveyard of that vanished church, which was dedicated to St. Mary of the Snows; the gracious gateway of Powis Lodge; the Firhill Well; the pleasance where the canons dwelt—the chanonry; that cathedral, the only one built of granite in our land; Downie's Pillar, with its strange story of the janitor who died of fear at a students' mock trial: the stone stair of the old bead-house; the doorway bearing the arms of Gavin Dunbar; and the six-hundred-year-old Brig of Balgownie.

> Though not a footfall echoes but your own
> You cannot walk down an old street alone.

I think if I were to pick out a companion of the noiseless footsteps with whom to walk through these streets of Old Aberdeen, I should choose a canon, and I'd like to go with him to his manse in the chanonry, and realize with him how that word, manse, was only a *lucus a non lucendo*; how here he had no abiding city, and how he must leave for his successor 'in the dining-hall, a large table, a silver spoon, a tablecloth and a towel. In the bedroom: a couch, a pair of linen sheets and two pairs of blankets. In the kitchen: an iron pot, an iron chain or kettle crook and a dish-clout!'

SKINNERGATE, PERTH

John G. Spence Smith

This old highway takes us in its name far back into the history of the crafts of the Scottish people, for it was William the Lion, who by Royal Charter admitted the skinners and glovers of Perth to the privileges of merchant-burgesses. Edward I stole that Charter, and it was lost with many other Scottish documents. The Skinnergate was the main entrance into Perth from the north before the bridge was built over the Tay, and the original wooden houses stood so close together that neighbours from the upper windows could shake hands across the street. On the High Street between the Skinnergate and the Kirkgate stood the old Cross. It was some twelve feet in height, and a set of steps inside it led to a balcony on the top. On the birthday of the Sovereign the loyal toasts were drunk on this balcony by the magistrates, and, as one early historian puts it, 'As each separate health was drunk, the bottles and glasses were thrown among the crowd, and new ones procured for the succeeding toast. So much for the civic economy of the day'. Ten years after the '45, traffic had increased to such an extent in Perth that both the old Cross and the city gates were removed.

Part of the work of the skinners and glovers was the manufacture of buckskin breeches. In fact a trade-sign of members of the Corporation was a pair of breeches with a buck between the legs. Writing in 1836, Mr. George Penny states :

'Besides the trade of gloves and breeches, the glovers carried on an extensive business in dressing sheep and goat skins, and employed a number of hands on their extensive premises beside the mill lade, which they still retain, where a few individuals do a little in the skin trade. The goat skins were dressed with the hair on, and sent to the London market with the sheep skins, where they were used for knapsacks for the army, and for covering saddles. Several individuals concerned in the trade made large sums of money. One old glover built a house on the side of the lade where the spinning mill stands, and put upon it as a motto—"Wha would have thought it, the skins would have bought it". To this trade was attached a manufacture of glue from the scrapings of the skins, but this has gone with the glove trade.'

David Peacock, another Perth historian, tells us that 'the last mortal relic of the operative glovers—a respectable old lady, Mrs. Prop—died in the Skinnergate' in 1846. But the Corporation has been immortalized by Sir Walter Scott in the person of that lady 'Catherine or Katie Glover, who was universally acknowledged to be the most beautiful young woman of the city or its vicinity, and whose renown, as the Fair Maid of Perth, had drawn on her much notice from the young gallants of the Royal Court'.

STIRLING BRIDGE

James Miller

If you possess an imagination, you can stand on this old Bridge of Stirling and hear the sound of saws and axes as they weaken its fore-runner, the old wooden bridge, in the year 1297. Those tools are handled by the men of William Wallace and Andrew Moray. Only two knights can ride abreast across this bridge, and when it has been sufficiently weakened for their purpose, the Scots retire to a position with the rest of the army on the slopes of the Abbey Craig, where the Wallace Monument stands to-day. Surrey, the commander of the English forces, arrives with his troops at the south end of the bridge, and bivouacs for the night. Next morning a division of English infantry cross the bridge, and Surrey—still on the south side—calls on Wallace to surrender. He is told that the Scots are there to fight. So he sends more troops across the bridge. When some half of the English have crossed, the English cavalry charge. And at that moment Wallace orders forward a large body of men whom he has held on his left flank. They take the English on the right flank close to the bridge, cut through them, and complete the demolition of the bridge. The English cavalry charge fails, and soon Surrey's troops to the north of the bridge are cut to pieces, while their commander on the south bank is unable to help. He starts the habit of flight to Berwick, which is later developed by Edward II and later still by Sir John Cope.

And, as I write of Sir John Cope, I recall another incident, this time in connection with this old Bridge of Stirling of Mr. Miller's picture. It is a fiction, but has all the quality of a fact. Davie Balfour and Alan Breck have reached the Carse of Stirling in their fugitive *Kidnapped* days, and here's part of Davie's story of Stirling Bridge:

'I was for pushing straight across; but Alan was more wary.

' "It looks unco' quiet," said he; "but for all that we'll lie down here cannily behind a dyke and make sure."

' So we lay for about a quarter of an hour, whiles whispering, whiles lying still and hearing nothing earthly but the washing of the water on the piers. At last there came by an old hobbling woman with a crutch stick. . . .

' "She's bound to be across now," I whispered.

' "Na," said Alan, "her foot still sounds boss upon the bridge."

'And just then—"Who goes?" cried a voice, and we heard the butt of a musket rattle on the stones. . . .

' "This'll never do," said Alan. "This'll never, never do for us, David."

'And without another word, he began to crawl away through the fields.'

THE OLD MILL, FIELD OF BANNOCKBURN

James Wright

Bannockburn in memory is more a matter of time and incident than of fact and place. From that Sunday, the twenty-third day of June in 1314, the thunder of De Bohun's charger, the crash of Bruce's battle-axe, as it breaks after its passage through the English knight's helmet and head, the words of old Ingelram de Umfraville, as he gazed on the Scots kneeling while the Abbot of Inchaffray passed along their line holding a crucifix before their eyes, to his contemptuous King: 'They ask for mercy, but not of you. These men will win all or die!' ring across six hundred years. But to get at facts and place is a different story. Research over the centuries has cut down the numbers engaged, and has finally proved that the battle could not have taken place on the traditional ground claimed as the Field of Bannockburn.

When Bruce knew that Edward was advancing to the relief of Stirling Castle he lined up his troops in the New Park behind the Bannock Burn, with two morasses, Milton Bog and Halbert's Bog, guarding each flank. He joined up the open space between those bogs with his stake-armoured pits. Randolph with his footmen (some five hundred pikes) acted as a kind of mobile reserve, and Sir Robert Keith with all the cavalry (some five hundred lances) was on the right. The English drew up their line on the other side of the Bannock, but contented themselves that day with an attack by heavy cavalry on the Scottish left. Randolph smashed them. Then came the De Bohun incident, and that was all the Sunday work. On the Sunday night Edward appears to have moved his troops across the Bannock, and drawn them up facing west in a position with the Forth round two sides, and the Bannock to the south. Bruce also moved his troops so as to face the English, who opened the ball with a cavalry charge. It broke on the Scottish spears. On the other hand a Scots cavalry flank charge smashed the English bowmen and slingers. The English found themselves hemmed in by river and burn and could not manoeuvre. The arrows of the Scots took frightful toll of the milling mass of the enemy, and sword and pike continued the good work. Edward fled to the castle, but de Mowbray, the English Governor, would not give him admittance. So the English King took a straight line for Dunbar, Douglas hard on his heels. He could never have made Stirling Castle if the battle had been fought on the traditional field. But that matters little, for, as we say in Scotland, 'it was here or hereaboots', and 'it was a famous victory'.

But visitors have come and always will come to the field where the Borestone stands, and thrill to the memories.

A SPEYSIDE CROFT

Alexander Macpherson

I was wandering one day along an old, old highway which runs above a tributary of the Spey. It was long since traffic had moved across this road, and the turf-covering was pleasant to the feet. Then suddenly I came on the croft-house. It was built right in the middle of the forgotten highway. In fact you approached it over an old bridge which carried the road of yesterday across a stream. My companion and I were examining this bridge when the crofter himself appeared, a powerfully built young fellow with flaxen hair and clear blue eyes. He was very polite in his address. 'Are you,' he asked, 'by any chance surveyors?' We explained that we were not; that we were two people just interested in the old road. 'Oh,' he said, still polite, but obviously very disappointed, 'I thought they might have been going to do something about the old road; make it so that we could use it.' He had been joined now by his wife, a girl as beautiful as a spring morning, with teeth like snow. With her was a little tow-haired boy of some five years, and in her arms a baby girl. 'They dinna want us here!' continued the crofter; and at that moment, a cock-grouse, his comb as red as fire, craicked at us in derision, and his 'Go-back! go-back!' sounded much more like 'Quite right! quite right!' And as I look at Mr. MacPherson's beautiful picture of a Speyside croft which might have been wiped out by a German bomb, I think of my crofter and his wife and bairns, and wonder if they were wiped out by a cock-grouse. They wouldn't be put out of the croft, of course; they would just have to go out because nothing was done about keeping it in a condition that would make it worth while for the crofter to remain. Well, well, Australia or Canada will gain what Scotland has lost. Yet love of place will remain, and I have no doubt that tow-haired laddie will join up in defence of the land which he had to leave, willy-nilly, should that land be threatened by some other foreign bomb.

A Shepherd's Croft
Sketch Macpherson
'62

TORPHICHEN CHURCH

James Miller

From the window of the room in St. Andrews, in which I am writing these notes, I can see gardens and buildings which occupy land which was once the property of the Knights of St. John. So, as I look at Mr. Miller's picture of the honest Parish Kirk of Torphichen, I remember that it, too, occupies a site that belonged to the same Order, and, if we enter the church, we shall find the tomb of Sir Walter Lindsay, the second-last Preceptor. But all that is left of the original church of his Preceptory are the choir and transepts. It is on the site of the nave that the present church stands, and it has been suggested that the upper stones of the tower were at one time part of the 'Hospital'. The present Parish Church, with its bleak blank north wall, and the large chimney that surmounts its crow-stepped gable, cannot claim the 'grace' of its forebear. There is another chimney on the south gable of the tower, and in the north-west corner a spiral staircase. There is, however, a twelfth-century chancel arch. The interior of the church is not particularly attractive, for the bare wall-space is not relieved by any ornamentation. There is a builder's drawing on the west wall of the south transept. In the churchyard is an interesting stone. It looks like an ordinary mile-stone, but there is a cross carved upon its top. This stone marked the centre of a sanctuary, the perimeter of which was indicated by similar stones each a mile distant from that centre. Not only the church, but all the ground inside the circle was sanctuary for the hunted deer of human kind— debtors and other unfortunates.

The 'sair sanct' gave this ground to the Knights Templar, and when that body was banned, the Knights of St. John succeeded to the property. But many of the leaders died in battles which had little connection with Jerusalem. Alexander de Wells, the Prior in Wallace's time (and Edward's man), was slain at Falkirk; Sir Henry Knolls, James IV's Preceptor, fell at Flodden. Later Preceptors displayed other qualities. Knoll's successor, Sir George Dundas, was at school with Hector Boece, and was a man of considerable learning and culture, while his successor, Sir William Lindsay, became Scotland's Justice-General. The last Preceptor, Sir James Sandilands, threw in his lot with the Reformers in 1560, bought the estates, and was created Lord Torphichen. Robert Hodge was the first Presbyterian minister of the Parish, and entered into his duties in 1572. But it was not much of a sanctuary for the first half-dozen incumbents, who seemed to have been manhandled frequently by their parishioners, and, on one occasion, the military had to be called in to assist the minister against his flock.

SOUTH OF EDINBURGH

Artists

A. E. BORTHWICK

MARJORIE E. BORTHWICK

MAY M. BROWN

ANNA DIXON

W. M. FRAZER

MARTIN HARDIE

P. MACKIE

ELIZABETH G. MOLYNEAUX

CHARLES OPPENHEIMER

ALEXANDER N. PATERSON

G. P. H. WATSON

JAMES WRIGHT

BORTHWICK CASTLE

A. E. Borthwick

'Ad construendam castrum in loco illo qui vulgariter dicitur le Mote de Lochorwart.' So runs the charter under the Great Seal which James I granted to Sir William Borthwick in 1430. Five hundred years have passed since this Borthwick Castle was built above the junction of Gore Water and the North Middleton Burn in the vicinity of Dalkeith, and, except for the destruction of part of the curtain wall, the great Keep remains much the same as when Sir William took up his residence in it. The base of the building is some seventy feet square, and on the west side there is a curious division in the centre of the thirteen-feet-thick walls (which soar to ninety feet of height) constructed probably so that more light could enter the main state rooms. A drawbridge gave access to those rooms, the chief of which—the great hall—is described as being so large that 'a man on horseback might turn a spear in it with all the ease imaginable'. It is not difficult to see great logs ablaze in the mighty fireplace and to hear the music coming from the musicians' gallery. But a lonely ghost paces the wide floor—the ghost of Mary, Queen of Scots. It is a June night of the year 1567. Morton and his friends have surrounded Borthwick Castle, in which Mary and her husband, Bothwell, have halted on their way to the Borders. Bothwell slips out, and makes his own escape in the darkness. Mary is left alone, 'so quiet that there was none with her passing six or seven persons'. Morton and his folk return to Edinburgh. Mary, the Queen, dresses as a man, and, booted and spurred, rides away to meet Bothwell, only to see him ride away from her for the last time at Carberry Hill. One hundred years later John, Eighth Lord Borthwick, defended his castle against Cromwell, and finally surrendered it to the Protector's forces. It remained untenanted for over a century and a half.

CAT ROW, DUNBAR

May M. Brown

This picture differs from the others in the volume in that it is a record of human dwellings which have gone for ever. Fisher quarters, old cellars, an old pier, and the Rock House on the right, all are gone. So are the cats which gave the Row its name. Here, where the fishwives cleaned fish and baited lines, there was a grand living for the tribes of Bubastis, and, when they desired a change of diet, round holes had been cut to admit them into the granaries which backed on the Row, and where rodents abounded. Since Cromwell's time (the Protector handed over £300 to build a harbour) they fished hard from this port, and the herring were plentiful. But the day arrived when the herring sought other grounds, and the fishing died. And why? you ask. Well, many reasons are given, but the most Scottish of them is that the whole failure results from the fact that, in the older days, despite the warnings of the Kirk, Dunbar men would go fishing on the Sabbath.

Mary M. Brown

FERNIEHIRST CASTLE

James Wright

In September 1803, with the assistance of William Laidlaw, Walter Scott conducted Dorothy and William Wordsworth over Ferniehirst Castle, where the Lake poet admired 'the grove of stately ancient elms above and below the ruin'. And a gruesome tale Scott and Laidlaw between them would have to tell. Sometime in the middle of the fifteenth century Sir Thomas Ker built the original castle 'marvelous strongly within a great wood'. That castle fell into the hands of the English in the dreich days after Pinkie, and the succeeding horror-story of rape, torture, and murder on the part of the Southerners is perhaps best left untold, as is the vengeance that the folk of the Forest of Jed took in their turn on the invaders. French troops aided Ker and his Borderers to win back the castle in 1549, but it was partially destroyed by Sussex's men in 1570, and further damaged two years later by Lord Ruthven and his followers. In 1598 was erected the building as it stands to-day, and which, curiously enough, has little of a war-like appearance. The castle is built in the form of an L, and from the old doorway a straight stair led to the first floor, and from it a wheel-stair to the two upper floors. The long wing of the house had originally vaulted cellars on the ground floor and a sequence of rooms entering one from the other on the upper floors. The Lothian Lords occupied the house till the middle of the eighteenth century, when much reconstruction was done. Ivy was removed from the outer walls, the inner ones were re-panelled, and the roof was put to rights, and when Dorothy Wordsworth made her notes it was 'inhabited by farmers'. 'The valley of the Jed is very solitary immediately under Ferniehirst', continues the lady. 'We walked down the river, wading almost up to the knees in fern, which in many parts overspread the forest ground.' I think those four old ghosts now will stand aside, and smile happily, as the latest occupants of Ferniehirst, the lasses and lads that go youth-hostelling, make their way laughing and singing to the old castle, the predecessor of which knew so much of tears and sorrow.

HERMITAGE CASTLE

Marjorie E. Borthwick

No mind 'innocent and quiet' ever took this grim place 'for an hermitage'. In a morass of Liddesdale desolation the great double tower of Hermitage rises, and its story is as grim as its physical appearance. The first peel was built in 1243, and some of the remains of it are embodied in the fifteenth-century structure which has withstood the ravages of five hundred years. Comyns—of that family to which Bruce's Dumfries victim belonged—first owned the castle, but, by the time Bruce was busy with his letters to the Pope in the Abbey of Aberbrothwock, Sir William de Soulis was the owner. A brutal man this Soulis to whom tradition has accorded a brutal passing, for the story goes that the poor people, who suffered under his lordship, seized him, took him to the Nine Stane Rig beside the castle, and there boiled him alive. But history gives him a somewhat easier death, for, in fact, he died a prisoner in Dumbarton Castle, where Bruce had thrown him, after he had made an attempt to usurp the throne of King Robert. Grahams held Hermitage, and then there came another unpleasant owner in the person of Douglas, Knight of Liddesdale, who threw Sir Alexander Ramsay of Dalhousie into his dungeon and left him there to starve to death. Above that dungeon was a granary and for a little while Sir Alexander kept his feeble spark of life aglow by eating the grains of corn which trickled through to his prison. James IV handed over the castle to the Hepburns, and the most picturesque story connected with Hermitage is that of the visit of Mary, Queen of Scots, to Bothwell recovering from a wound dealt him by Elliot of Park, when Hepburn had been going about his lawful occasions as Warden of the Marches. Twenty miles rode the Queen to see her champion. Twenty miles back to Jedburgh she rode in the rain and the wind. Gloomy Hermitage almost claimed another victim, for the Queen was attacked by fever, and many feared, and not a few hoped, that she would die. On that ride her horse sank deep into what is still named 'The Queen's Mire'. Many years afterwards a little spur was found there. Did it once belong to the most romantic lady in all Scottish history? And so to something else that was lost. On 23rd September 1831, Sir Walter Scott left Abbotsford for London. On the way south in one of the inns in which he stayed he lost a ring which he usually wore. It had been dug out of the ruins of Hermitage Castle, and, writes Lockhart, 'it had probably belonged of yore to one of the "Dark Knights of Liddesdale". The ring, which is a broad belt of silver, with an angel holding the Heart of Douglas, was found, and is now worn by Mr. Morritt.'

LINLITHGOW PALACE COURTYARD

Alexander N. Paterson

Here the Sair Sanct and England's Edward came;
Each built a house of wood which died in flame.
Here Scotland's poet-king a dwelling made
Of stone with slates from Angus quarries laid.
His son sent fisherman that loch to try
For wriggling eels to make a tasty pie
To tempt the appetite of his fair Queen.
And in this Scots Decameron demesne
His grandson sat beside his royal bride
While the Black Death raxed Scotland far and wide.
Here the fourth James lazed at his kingly ease
Among his flower-beds and his honey-bees,
Playing sometimes the leech, sometimes the flute,
While eighteen carts creaked here from Holyrood
Bringing Royal Margaret's wardrobe. Here she kneeled
And prayed for James far off on Flodden Field.
Here a December baby's first faint cry
Swelled to undying Scottish history.
That lass, here first beheld the light of day,
Who was to see it pass in Fotheringay.
Here sick in mind and body, dull and glum,
Mooned James, that 'wisest fool in Christendom'.
Here each romantic matron and each maid
Donned the Royal Tartan and the White Cockade
To welcome Charlie, while that fountain fine
Splashed that same courtyard red with ruby wine.
Here came the Butcher's crew one cold spring day,
Fired their straw bedding when they went away,
And the murk flames left but this ruin hoary
To tell a Palace's romantic story.

"LINLITHGOW PALACE" COURTYARD   Alexander N Paterson

THE CHURCH OF HADDINGTON

P. Mackie

In the reign of Alexander II, a Franciscan Monastery was founded in Haddington, and John Major tells us it was known as 'Lucerna Laudoniae'—the Lamp of Lothian. A light was ever kept burning in its lofty choir, which in the darkness of the night shone out, a guiding star for pilgrims. It is claimed by some authorities that the present Haddington parish church is built on the same foundation as that of the Franciscan Monastery. This church takes a place among the very best fifteenth-century Scottish buildings. The choir is in ruins, and it is the nave (210 feet long by 62 feet broad) in which the worshippers now congregate. The church is cruciform, and above the transept the central tower, with its large three-light windows on each of the four sides, soars 90 feet into the air. The crown, which was similar to that on St. Giles, Edinburgh, has been removed. The fabric is a red freestone.

Within sight of this church John Knox is said to have been born, and his doctrines were made the excuse for the destruction of much of the beauty of this church, although the English invaders had a hand in that as well. The eastern part was unroofed at the time of the Reformation, the window arches broken, altars, figures of saints and angels pulled down or defaced; but the Maitlands, to whom the church lands were dispensed, put a stop to the vandalism, and people began to worship in the nave. In 1811 very considerable repairs to that part of the church were completed.

There are many interesting stones in the churchyard raised to the memory of Lauderdales and Elchos. There are two at which the reader may care to halt with me for a moment. The one is an obelisk to the memory of that remarkable orphaned herd-laddie of Carpowin, Perthshire, John Brown, who, though he never had a teacher, made himself proficient in Latin, Greek, Hebrew, French, Italian, German and the languages of Arabia, Syria, Persia and Ethiopia. Brown gave up his herding to become a pedlar. Then he set himself up as a schoolmaster at Gairney Bridge, near Kinross, in that school in which, at a later date, Michael Bruce was to teach. Brown became one of the 1733 seceders, took training under the Associate Synod, and in 1750 was licensed to preach. He was elected minister to the Secession Congregation in Haddington. Later, when a Professor of Divinity under the Synod, he published his *Dictionary of the Holy Bible* and *The Self-Interpreting Bible*. They wanted him to preach in New York, but he did not accept the invitation. He died at Haddington in 1787.

The other stone covers the shell that once contained the restless vigorous spirit of that lady who, in 1823, said to Thomas Carlyle: 'Your friend I will be . . . but your wife never.' And yet in 1826 she became Jane Welsh Carlyle.

DOOCOT AT PRESTONKIRK

W. M. Frazer

It was the habit of boys in my native place to possess each a catapult, made from the fork of a branch of a tree, strong rubber, and a piece of leather. Their range was a doocot, and their targets the pigeons which entered and left the many holes. There were little ledges at the entrances to these holes, and it was when the pigeon landed on a ledge that you got in your shot. The pigeons became very knowledgeable, and actually they used to close their wings in their flight and enter the holes without making any use whatever of the landing-place. The 'bags' were generally non-existent.

That children must have always been in the habit of making attacks on Scots doocots is proved by the fact that a Statute of 1503 declares that 'the breaking of dovecots is a point of dittay (indictment)'. Fathers and mothers of children guilty of that offence were liable to a fine of 13s. 4d. Scots for each of the children, 'or else to deliver them up to the Judge to be scourged according to the fault'. In 1579, by a further Statute, the breakers of dovecots were given eight days' imprisonment and fed on bread and water for a first offence; if they repeated it a third time, they were 'hanged to the death'. People who were found shooting at pigeons for a second time had the right hand cut off.

As far back as the year 1503, every lord and laird was ordained to erect dovecots. But one hundred years later, so greatly had the pigeon colony increased, that the birds became a public nuisance, and an Act was passed in 1617 enacting that 'no person shall have power or liberty to build a dovecot upon any lands within the realm, neither within Burgh nor in the Country, except he have lands and teinds pertaining to him, extending in yearly rent to ten chalders victual'.

Dr. John Thomson, who was minister of Markinch in 1800, writes in his *General View of the Agriculture of the County of Fife*:

'Pigeons, however much esteemed as an article of food, and however ready and convenient a dish they may afford to the table, are justly reckoned a great nuisance to the country at large. There are, in this County (Fife), not fewer perhaps than 360 pigeon-cotes, which may contain 36,000 pairs of breeders. They make dreadful havoc among the grain, particularly the wheat and pease, in filling and harvesting time, and are supposed to consume not less than between 3,000 and 4,000 bolls of grain annually.'

The Doocot at Prestonkirk is of the sixteenth-century bee-hive type. The string-courses running round the walls were constructed as a protection against rats. Inside these doocots the nests were made of stone-slabs, and you got to them by climbing what was known as a 'potence', a revolving beam stretching from floor to roof with rungs at various levels.

MELROSE ABBEY

G. P. H. *Watson*

No building in all our land has suffered so often the attacks of enemies; yet no ruin has retained so much of beauty, or burgeoned anew in so kindly a second spring created for it by the wand of a magician. The original building, founded by David I in 1136, was completely destroyed by fire ten years later; its successor was burned by Edward II; Robert the Bruce rebuilt it; Richard II set fire to it in 1378. During the reigns of Henry VIII, Edward VI, and Elizabeth, it was harried time and again; much of it was destroyed in 1544; twice it was pillaged by the English in 1545; and finally, as one writer puts it,

'In 1569, the nobility of Scotland and their military retainers, under the sacred name of the Reformation, and with an unjust reflection of the odium they incurred on John Knox and his fellow reformers, completed by pillage, defacement and dilapidation what the English had left to be done in order to the conversion of the pile into an unroofed, gutted, partially overthrown, and altogether yawning ruin.'

But nought could altogether destroy the beauty of the workmanship of the Cistercian monks. They took the Scots kale leaf as the model for the decoration of the capitals on the columns—

> And the pillars with cluster'd shafts so trim
> With base and with capital flourish'd around,
> Seemed bundles of lances which garlands had bound.

As Sir D. Y. Cameron wrote in *The Artist*:

'All must be seen and lingered with to be fully enjoyed. The hidden corner, no less than the sunlit, must be studied till all the ornaments are known and loved. How perfect is the workmanship; no slipshod, no shoddy, no fine carving wasted on poor stone, but all the stones laid in as found in the quarries, and hence a minimum of decay.'

So to the second spring in the genius of Sir Walter Scott. Here was the centre of his land. Here waved he the wizard's wand to greatest purpose, and the abbey came to life anew in his novels and poems, and to a life of greater intensity than before, for it is Scott's Melrose which lives all over the world—it is Scott's Melrose folk come to see. It is the light of his genius that—

> Streams on the ruined central tower:
> When buttress and buttress alternately
> Seemed framed of ebon and ivory,
> When silver edges the imagery,
> And the scrolls that teach thee to live and die.

Somehow then, it seems right that Tom Purdie should sleep here, that Peter Mathieson should sleep here—close to Bruce's heart, and all that's left of Douglas of Chevy Chase and of Michael Scot, of the race of the House of Zair and of Alexander II's Queen.

THE HIGH HOUSE, WANLOCKHEAD

Anna Dixon

It is said that only the love of gold could have driven anyone to go to such a bleak place as Wanlockhead, Dumfriess-shire's Ultima Thule. Some time in the middle of the sixteenth century a German prospector went away among those lonely hills searching—and found a little gold and much lead. Hence the name Leadhills. But the villages of Wanlockhead and Leadhills have one claim to fame. They are the highest villages in Scotland, Leadhills winning by four feet in its one thousand three hundred and eighty. Tomintoul, the next highest village, is over two hundred feet lower. For a long time the Youth Hostel at Tomintoul claimed to be the highest of such institutions, but they opened one at Wanlockhead, so that the Lowlands beat the Highlands for height as far as hostellers go. Which recalls how disappointed John Hill Burton was when he found that Ben Muich Dhui, his favourite mountain, had to take second place among the stars to Ben Nevis. He was on the top of Ben Nevis at the time, and he writes in his *Cairngorm Mountains* (published in 1864):

'Turning my eyes from the terrible fascinations of the precipice to the apex of the hill, now in full view, a strange sight there met them. . . . It was neither more nor less than a crowd of soldiers occupying nearly the whole table-land of the summit! . . . A very short sentence from the good-humoured-looking young fellow who received our first breathless and perplexed inquiry solved the mystery—"Did you never hear of the Ordnance Survey?" To be sure, everybody had heard of it: but the impression created concerning it was as of something like a mathematical line, with neither breadth nor thickness; but here it was in substantial operation. The party were occupied in erecting a sort of dwelling for themselves—half tent, half hut. . . .

'In the course of conversation with these new friends I alighted on a subject in which I had long taken an interest. They had already conducted some operations on Ben Muich Dhui, and they were now commencing such surveys on Ben Nevis as would enable them finally to decide which of these mountains had the honour of being the highest land in the United Kingdom. Competition had of late run very close between them: and the last accounts had shown Ben Muich Dhui only some twenty feet or so ahead. I freely confess to a preference for Ben Muich Dhui, which the recent decision against him has not mitigated—indeed, one is always bound to back one's favourite the more warmly if he is unfortunate, and driven from the eminence to which he has been entitled. The recollections of these things inclined me, even when standing on the rival's top, to put in a good word for Ben Muich Dhui; and before separating from these hermits of Her Majesty's Ordnance, I requested, if they had any influence in the matter, that they would "find" for my favourite.'

NEIDPATH CASTLE

Martin Hardie

I first saw Neidpath when I was a very small boy. With my father I climbed a stair into what, I believed, was the banqueting hall. The keeper's wife was washing clothes in a steaming tub which stood upon the floor. She was a most pleasant lady, but I had a sense of the desecration of the place. I saw the view from the top of the roof, but felt that the parapet was flimsy and unworthy of the place. Though it be but a legend, the story was told me then, and must always remain truth for me, of the maid, daughter of the House of March, who loved a son of the Laird of Tushielaw. But parents disapproved, the lad sought other lands, the maid wilted, the lover was recalled. But he rode past the castle, and did not recognize the lady, so much had sorrow changed her.

> The castle arch, whose hollow tone
> Returns each whisper spoken,
> Could scarcely catch the feeble moan,
> Which told her heart was broken.

It was many years later when I learned how 'Old Q', the fourth Duke of Queensbury, whose ancestors had purchased Neidpath, did all he could to wreck and destroy the place in the last decade of the eighteenth century. He cut down all the trees, old and young, disfigured everything, and tried to make a desert of it all. The money he received for the trees went to a natural daughter; the satisfaction he got was in despoiling his heir. Wordsworth came along, and calculated the incident was worth a sonnet, and designated the Duke 'Degenerate Douglas'. In many ways that was the end of the story of this grim building by the pleasant Tweed.

Neidpath was the most massive peel in the Shire of Peebles, and originally belonged to the Frasers, the last of them being that Sir Simon who licked the English so satisfactorily at Roslin Moor twelve years before Bannockburn. The property then passed to the Hays of Yester, and one of those Hays gallantly held the castle against Cromwell's artillery in 1650. Not till part of the castle had been cannoned to pieces did he surrender. Thirty-six years later the first Duke of Queensbury bought the estate—and that was that.

An Earl of Wemyss replanted the policies with trees, and now the castle is a quiet, pleasant place, sung to sleep from all its sorrows by the waters of Tweed.

NORMAN ARCHES, JEDBURGH ABBEY

Elizabeth G. Molyneaux

Eight hundred years ago the then Priory of Jedburgh was raised by David I to the dignity of an abbey, and the highlight in the first century and a half of its existence was the marriage of our third Royal Alexander to Iolande, daughter of the Count of Dreux, which with all the colour and pageantry of the times took place within its walls. Edward I, in his natural character, stripped the lead from the roof of the abbey and completely destroyed the conventual buildings in the year 1300, and in the fourteenth century 'during the long succession of international conflicts which followed the Peace of Northampton in 1328, the abbey rocked under the violent rush of invasion and repulse, and underwent many a desolating change'. Surrey and Hertford poured out their wrath on it in the sixteenth century, and it never recovered from a final destruction in 1545. In 1793, a wall was built within the ruins of the church to improve the conditions under which folk of the Reformed Faith were worshipping there. But in 1875 the Marquess of Lothian built another church, and the ruins were left to their slumbers. Authority has since treated them with reverent care.

Of the Norman style of architecture as exhibited in the arches of Jedburgh Abbey, Macgibbon and Ross write in their *The Ecclesiastical Architecture of Scotland*:

'The style is easily recognized by its simple and massive forms and its semi-circular arches. The exterior is generally plain, with broad and slightly projecting buttresses attached to the building and sometimes crowned with pinnacles. The doorways are, however, generally treated in a more ornamental manner. They are often deeply recessed, and have the jambs decorated with a series of round shafts set in square nooks or recesses with richly carved caps and bases. The arch mouldings, which are also numerous, are arranged in square steps or orders, and frequently ornamented with much carving of special kinds of enrichments. . . . The windows are wide in proportion to their height and are covered in with round arches. . . . Of the monastic foundations of St. Margaret and her sons we still retain the venerable Norman nave of Dunfermline and portions of the Norman edifices of Holyrood, Dryburgh and Jedburgh. . . . Holyrood, Jedburgh and St. Andrews contain much work of the period of transition from the Norman to the First Pointed style which came into use about the beginning of the thirteenth century.'

OLD ROWALLAN HOUSE

Alexander N. Paterson

Three miles north of the town of Kilmarnock by the side of peaceful Carmel Water and in the pleasant company of gracious trees, this old home of the Mures of Rowallan dovers and dreams its now uneventful years away. It is a dwelling of many parts, for its successive owners added to it as they thought fit and found necessary during the some five hundred years of its story, the highlight of which is that in the ruins to the left of the courtyard, which are all that is left of the first tower, there is every likelihood that Elizabeth Mure was born—Elizabeth Mure who was to marry Robert the High Steward, later King Robert II of Scotland, and was to become the ancestress of our present Sovereign, Elizabeth. Later builders extended the house round the courtyard, which has a knoll in the centre. The frontage, which is shown in the picture, and which consists of two string-coursed drum-towers with a doorway between them at the top of a flight of steps, was constructed in the middle of the sixteenth century by John Mure of Rowallan, and he and his lady, Marion Cuninghame, are remembered on a tablet bearing the date 1562 and carrying their family arms. As a crest appears the head of a Moor, which the editor of Timothy Pont's *Cunninghame* suggests as 'probably allusive of some feat performed during the Crusades against the Saracens; in the old Family Tree it seems alluded to in the "bludy heid".' He continues: 'In an ornamental compartment over the principal door, at the top of a long flight of steps, is cut in stone the Royal Arms of Scotland with the Supporters and Regal accompaniments surmounting the family shield.' The passage from that door leads right through to the courtyard, in the south wall bounding which is the entrance to the main hall, two public rooms, and a dining-room with a turret-stair giving access to the upper floor. Also in this block are a kitchen, cellars and the well. Facing this block is the ruined part of the house with another building of a later date, apparently a spare kitchen.

The Mures of Rowallan march with some colour across the stage of Scottish history. They appeared to have forfeited this property at an early date, but one of them fought at Largs in 1263 with such distinction that 'King Alexander did remunerate his valour with marriage of Isobel, only daughter and sole heir of Sir William Cumming of Rowallan'. This Mure was the great-great-grandfather of King Robert's queen. A Mure died beside his King at Flodden, and the last male heir, Sir William, fought under Gustavus Adolphus. His daughter married, as her second husband, Lord Boyle (later Earl of Glasgow). Their daughter succeeded to the Rowallan estates, and married Sir James Campbell, a son of an Earl of Loudoun. Campbell was killed at Fontenoy, and the property remained in Loudoun possession.

ROWALLAN CASTLE AYRSHIRE

SKETCH PLAN

WHITE GABLES, KIRKCUDBRIGHT

Charles Oppenheimer

The peal of bells from the old Tolbooth Tower by those white gables has been heard by many ears, and one family and two individuals come to the mind when considering this picture, out of the range of which is the Castle, with all its particular history of English invaders from Edward I to Cromwell, and of visits of the Stuart Kings. The family was that of the Lords of Kirkcudbright, and in the early years of the eighteenth century the then head of the house had fallen on such evil days that he opened a white gable as an alehouse, where his heir acted as boots, and his daughter as chambermaid. He, however, did not believe in cleaning windows, and would not supply Sunday dinner, so the venture was not a particular success. One of the individuals was a certain William Marshall. His body lies in the kirkyard under a stone which informs the passer-by:

THE REMAINS OF WM. MARSHALL, TINKLER, WHO DIED
28TH NOVEMBER 1792, AT THE ADVANCED AGE OF 120 YEARS.

And the second individual is that son of the gardener at Arbigland, who became known to the world as Paul Jones, and has been claimed as the United States of America's Nelson, George Preedy, in comparing Paul Jones and Nelson writes :

'The Scot is a far more attractive character than the Englishman, better looking, better mannered, possessed of more lofty ideals and finer feelings, as vain but not as neurotic, not so well born, yet not so vulgar; but he lacked the luck that set Horatio Nelson on the way where his genius was bound to shine, and he lacked that authority over his crews, that unquestioned position and that long-established orthodox patriotism which served Nelson so well.'

It has been pointed out by Mr. John Peacock that the fight between Jones's *Bonhomme Richard* and H.M.S. *Serapis* is undoubtedly the subject of that naval battle described by Walt Whitman in 'Song of Myself', and that Jones is described in the lines:

Serene stands the little Captain,
He is not hurried, his voice is neither high nor low,
His eyes give more light to us than our battle-lanterns.
Towards twelve, there in the beams of the moon, they surrender to us.

CHARLES OPPENHEIMER.